LANGPORT, THE HEART OF SOMERSET

Cover: View of Langport (photograph courtesy Julian Comrie);
Above: Houses on The Hill (drawing by Tony Haskell;
Overleaf: Langport from the air.

LANGPORT
The heart of Somerset

Heather Ridgway

WESSEX HOUSE PRESS

Published in 1994 by
Wessex House Press
Bow Street
Langport
Somerset

Design and typesetting by
Ex Libris Press
1 The Shambles
Bradford on Avon
Wiltshire

Typeset in 11 point Palatino

Printed and bound in Britain by
Cromwell Press
Broughton Gifford
Wiltshire

ISBN 0 9524730 0 3

I dedicate the book to Derrick, who might well have written a better one himself on the same subject, had he not suffered a stroke.

CONTENTS

Introduction   7

Chapter 1   Topography of Langport - River Parrett - Neolithic Times - Celts - *Belgae* - *Damnonii* - Roman Invasion - Villas - Roman withdrawal to 500 AD   11

Chapter 2   Saxon Invasion of Somerset - Battle of Llongborth - Cerdic - Cenwalch - Battle of Penselwood - Saxons in Langport - Centwine - Ine and his laws - founding of Muchelney Abbey - Langport part of Somerton royal manor. 500-800AD   19

Chapter 3   The arrival of the Danes - year of nine Battles - King Alfred - Danegeld - Athelney - Battle of Ethandune - Baptism of Guthrum - Treaty of Wedmore - Danelaw   25

Chapter 4   Burghal Hidage 912 AD - Langport as a borough (burh) - agricultural system - trade - market - Edward the Elder - Athelstan (925-940 AD) - Rebuilding of Muchelney Abbey - Langport granted a Mint   34

Chapter 5   'Frankpledge' - Church's influence - life of parish priest - Royal Hall in Langport - Langport's ancient Court - Hundred System - Ethelred the Unready (979-1017AD) - recommencement of Danish wars. 940-1066AD   42

Chapter 6   Norman Conquest - William I - Langport loses its Mint - Domesday Book - River Parrett - Langport's Moors - Henry I (1100-1135AD) Leper Hospital - Parish Church   47

Chapter 7   Henry II - Assize Legislation - Property Sales - Policing - Outlawry - Withy Growing and Auctions - Langport Manor given to Sir Richard Revel - Life in Langport 1154-1199AD   54

Chapter 8   The de Lortys, Langport's Lords of the Manor - Magna Carta - Merchant Guild - Hanging Chapel - Langport's Economic Position - Trade/Wool and Cloth - the de Montacutes - Black Death - Friars. 1199-1349AD   60

Chapter 9 The Beauforts Langport's Lords - Lollardry in Langport - War of Roses - Lady Margaret Beaufort - Henry VII - Perkin Warbeck Rebellion - Langport Fined. 1349AD - 1509AD   68

Chapter 10 Henry VIII. King's Commission - Reformation - Dissolution of Monasteries - Hanging Chapel becomes Town Hall - Mary - Elizabeth - Langport's Lord of the Manor executed for Treason - Langport reverts to the Crown - Langport granted a Charter by Elizabeth   73

Chapter 11 James I - Langport Granted a New Charter in 1616 - Details - the Bridges - Eels - Barge Trade - Langport's Inns - The Harshness of the Age   80

Chapter 12 Charles I - Revival of Law of Knighthood - Ship Money - Civil War (Royalists and Parliamentarians) - Battle of Langport, July 10th 1645 - Cromwell   87

Chapter 13 Cromwell, Lord Protector - Court of Survey of Langport Corporation's Tenants and Possessions - Restoration - Berkeleys Langport's Lords of the Manor - John Bush - Langport's Town School - Gillet Endowment - School Life   95

Chapter 14 James II. Monmouth Rebellion - Judge Jeffreys - Bloody Assize - Langport Men Hung and Quartered - William and Mary - Langport Signed Oath Roll - Langport Manor Update   101

Chapter 15 Langport School - Schoolmasters - Langport Corporation - Queen Anne - Coronation Day Celebrations - George I - George II - George III - Parish History - Social Life   109

Chapter 16 Years of Langport's Greatest Prosperity - William Pitt, the Elder - Pynsent Monument - Stuckey's Bank - Stuckey/Bagehot Partnership - Walter Bagehot - River Trade Flourishing - Lovibond's Railway   115

Chapter 17 Education - Quekett Family - 1815 Celebrations - Fishing - Markets - Amenities in Langport   123

Chapter 18 Finances - The Coming of the Railway - Decline of Waterborne Traffic - Langport a Borough no longer - The Future   132

Bibliography   143

INTRODUCTION

In producing this book, I have of necessity both consulted and quoted largely, in some cases word for word, from the works of many writers, both still alive and deceased, without whom these chapters may never have been written. It has not proved possible to obtain permission from everyone to do this. I merely hope the research they have carried out will continue to be recognised and acknowledged for an even longer period than might have been the case. I owe them a great debt in their exploring and keeping alive the history of the times we live in. In spite of having said this, I should mention specifically the work of Robin Bush and Dr. Robert Dunning in connection with *The Victoria History of the County of Somerset, Vol.III*, from which I have quoted unashamedly, but I found any work on the topic of Langport would be incomplete without reference to such a comprehensive document.

A special warm note of thanks to Brian Denman, without whose immediate and enthusiastic help all this would have taken much longer to make a reality.

I am grateful to the following for permission to use their photographs, maps and drawings: Douglas Allen Photography, the Admiral Blake Museum, Mrs Shirley Brown, Brian Denman, Tony Haskell, Gina Langford, Edward Paget-Tomlinson, Derek Phillips, the Somerset Archaeological and Natural History Society, Somerset County Council Library Service, Alun Walters, Robert Webb and the National Portrait Gallery.

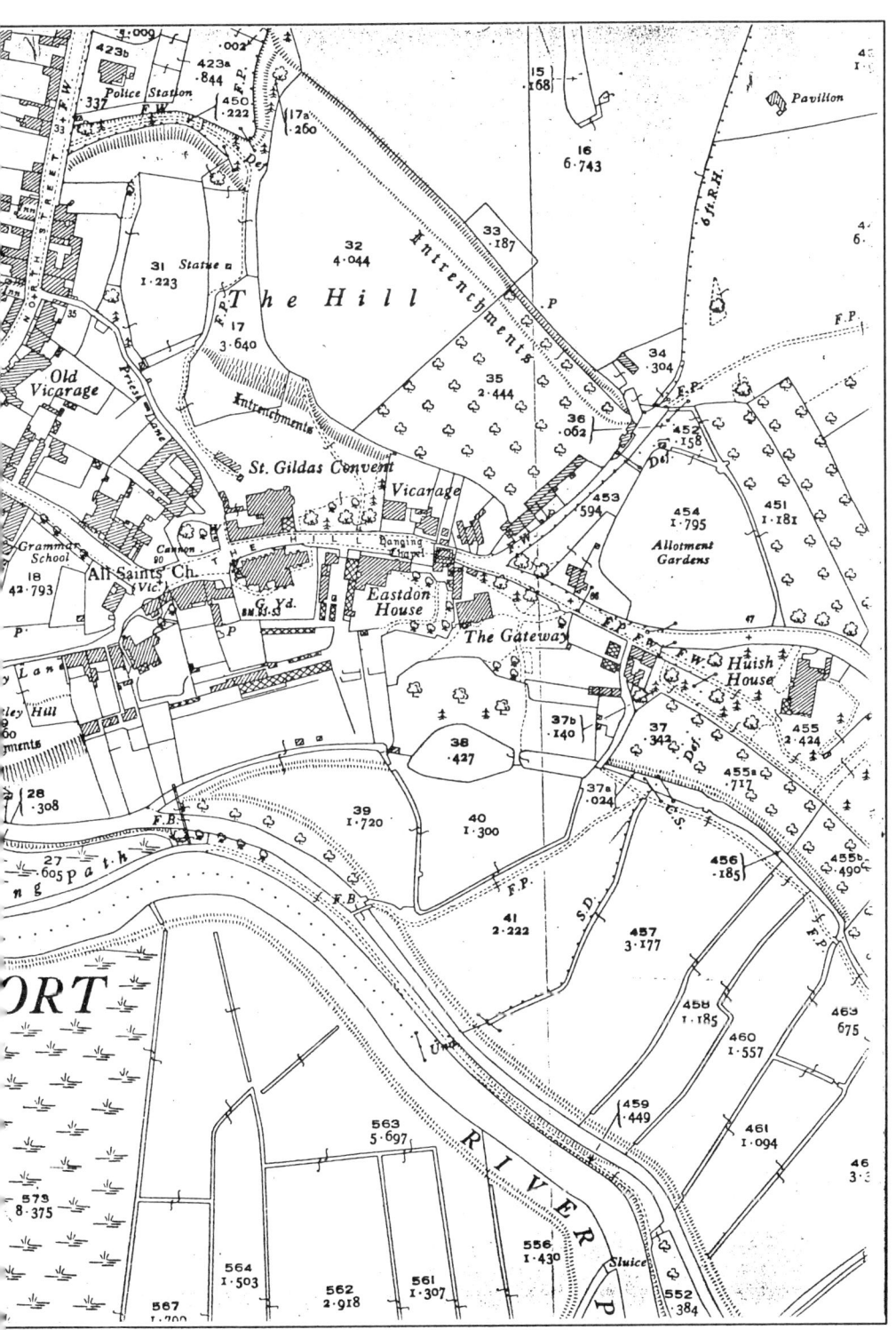

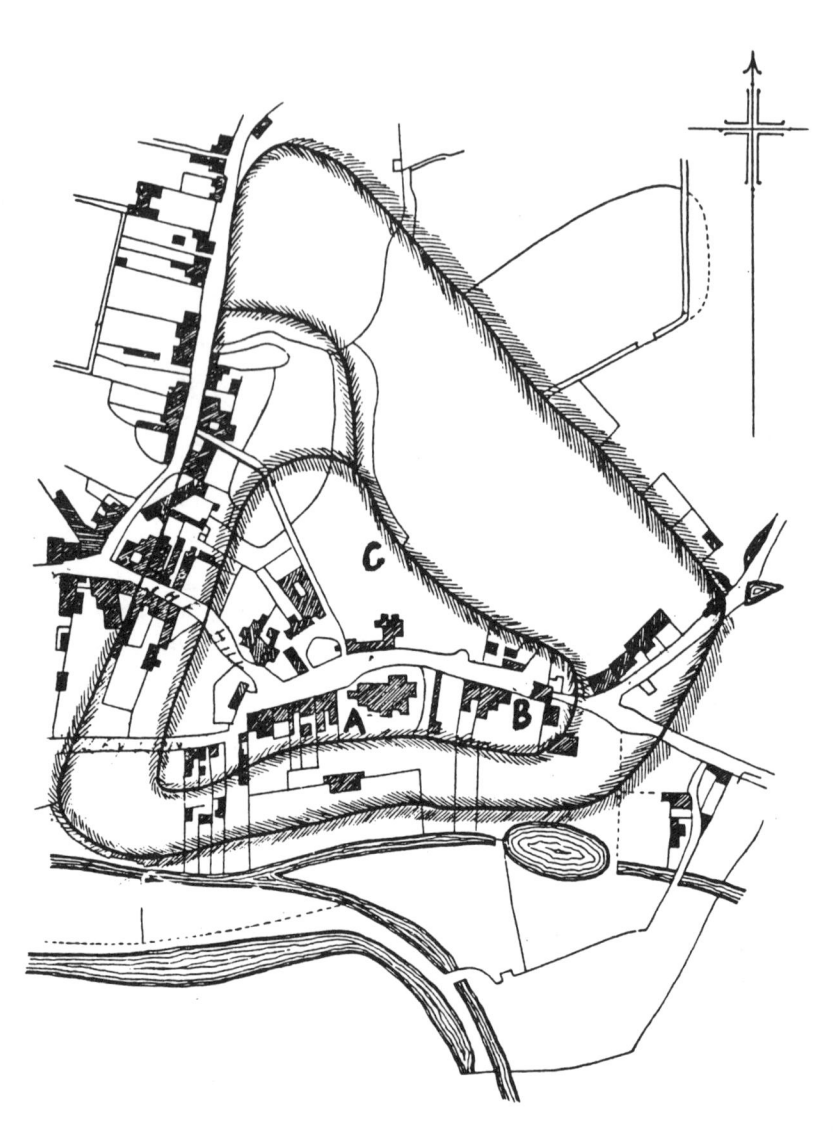

A. Church   B. Hanging Chapel   C. Enclosure

Pre-Roman Earthworks in Langport

Chapter 1

Topography of Langport - River Parrett - Neolithic Times - Celts - Belgae - Damnonii - Roman Invasion - Villas - Roman withdrawal ... to 500AD

Langport Parish, a tiny, quaint town in Somerset where Briton, Roman, Saxon, and Norman have succeeded each other, is an irregularly shaped region north and east of a bend in the River Parrett. It is almost surrounded by Huish Episcopi near the junction of three Sedgemoor rivers – the Parrett, which is tidal, the Isle and the Yeo. It lies five miles west of Somerton, two miles to the north of Muchelney, and thirteen miles from each of Taunton, Bridgwater, Yeovil, Crewkerne and Glastonbury, with a population of not more than a thousand. Langport is set where West Sedgemoor merges into King's Sedgemoor, surrounded by long, level meadows intersected by wide rhines. Sometimes it has an atmosphere characteristic of Sedgemoor – the same indescribable blue haze which invests the moors.

It is possible that the oldest reference to *Llongborth* was made by the British poet, Llywarch Hen, a prince of Cumberland (496-646AD). But it is difficult to identify this word (meaning a harbour with ships) with Langport, and the detail remains unproven. In Domesday, Langport is spelt *Lanporth* and as such would mean 'Church at Harbour'. *Lamport, Langeport, Longport* and *Lanporda* are common forms in other documents. In the years of Henry VI (1422AD), there was mention of *Langporte Eastoverne* and *Westoverne*, being references to Langport's position by the Parrett – the river which has played such an important role in its history.

Langport Hill rise from the moors in the east and is separated by about half a mile from Hurd's Hill in the west. In the rainy weeks of winter, even in these days of good drainage, it is possible to stand on Langport Hill and see the whole countryside under water for miles, sometimes for many weeks. To the south-west lies Whatley Hill, a small spur above the river.

The whole valley of the Parrett has been raised across the years by river deposits. Banks of sea sand against the slight elevations of the valley, show clearly how they were once washed by sea waves. Near Crandon Bridge the alluvial deposit was eight to ten feet deep over the peat at one time. It is very likely the ford which existed in the River Parrett, where today exists Bow Bridge, was one of the most frequented tracks in these parts used by Neolithic men, summer only assumed. Their remains have been discovered on both sides of Langport, at Sparkford, at Taunton, and at Staple Fitzpaine. The tidal waters of the Parrett would have been a natural highway for their expeditions to the Severn Sea and Wales, and it is possible they were the first to dig out earthworks, both on Langport Hill and Hurd's Hill.

It has been said the population in Neolithic times was large. Tribes lived in definite centres, occupied with agriculture, and subsisting to a lesser degree by hunting and fishing. Besides weaving, spinning and pottery, and mining for flints, they could build boats, and they bartered. The people themselves were swarthy – about five-feet five-inches in height. Some would have been clad in linen, others in skins, ornamented with necklaces and pendants of stone, bone or pottery. They would have had stone axes with lethally sharp edges fixed in wooden handles, and little saws made of carefully notched pieces of flint, split with stone wedges.

It is supposed the Celtic conquerors, with their metal weapons, followed the Neolithic period after some long intervals, and that the *Belgae*, a warlike and aggressive tribe from Gaul, who had over-run East Somerset before the end of the third century BC lived on Langport Hill. The *Damnonii*, called this by the Romans, were a tribe of Britons living in Devon and its environments, and on Hurd's Hill.

With the Roman invasion begins the historic period in Britain. About ninety years after Caesar's failure to occupy the country, it was successfully conquered about 43AD. During this long time, the British became more civilized and educated, and had grown familiar with Roman ways. We shall never know in what manner Roman legionaries first crossed Langport ford and occupied the earthworks. The first attraction to draw the Romans so far west was probably Mendip lead, and it seems possible in Roman times the rewards of agriculture were sufficiently great to make it worthwhile to attack the forests which covered this part of the county, and to settle on what must have been productive land once it had been cleared. Also there must have been a great demand for fuel to supply the elaborate heating systems in their houses.

In spite of doubt expressed as to whether Bow Street owes it existence to the Romans or not, the needs of the district in those years must have required such a roadway, not only as a route from the West Country to London. Langport was in an area of numerous Roman villas. There were two dwellings at Drayton and one at Bawdrip. A villa at Low Ham had two mosaic pavements. One depicted the story of Dido and Aeneas, which is now on view in the County Museum at Taunton. And the *Belgae* on Langport Hill would hardly grieve when Vespasian and his son Titus, who slowly broke the forces of the two 'mighty nations' of the south and west, put a yoke on their old adversaries, the *Damnonii*, and planted an outpost in Westover.

Although there have been scattered traces of Roman occupation in our area, the greater part was never fully settled. Yet it is hard to believe that the Romano-British of that prosperous age of road and bridge building, would be content not to construct a thoroughfare through Langport rather than leave the area unattended and flooded six months of the year, with ensuing difficulties of communication. Whatever the truth, Bow Street possibly a natural track in the first place, must have been built as it now stands, supported on arches to allow the free passage of water of the moors from the upper to lower side.

For nearly four centuries Roman rule continued in Britain and was on the whole advantageous. The Romans had found the land encumbered with forests and marshes. Towns were nothing but huts surrounded by stockaded earthworks in forest clearings. Tribes were occupied in perpetual warfare one against the other. The Romans changed the face of the country. Their roads, bridges and fords joined towns together all the year round. They established a form of peace and justice among the people, and compelled quarrelling tribes to settle their differences in law courts. On the other hand, Roman burdens of taxation and enlistment fell heavily on the province.

The decline of Roman power necessitated the withdrawal of their troops from Britain about 410AD. At that time the signs of the coming storm of Saxon invasion were very clear, and the numbers of Roman villas in our neighbourhood would be a great draw to the savage raiders who in the early years, fearing magic, destroyed statues and broke up mosaic pavements in search of treasure they suspected to be hidden underneath.

It may be worthwhile to consider what the Roman villas were like –

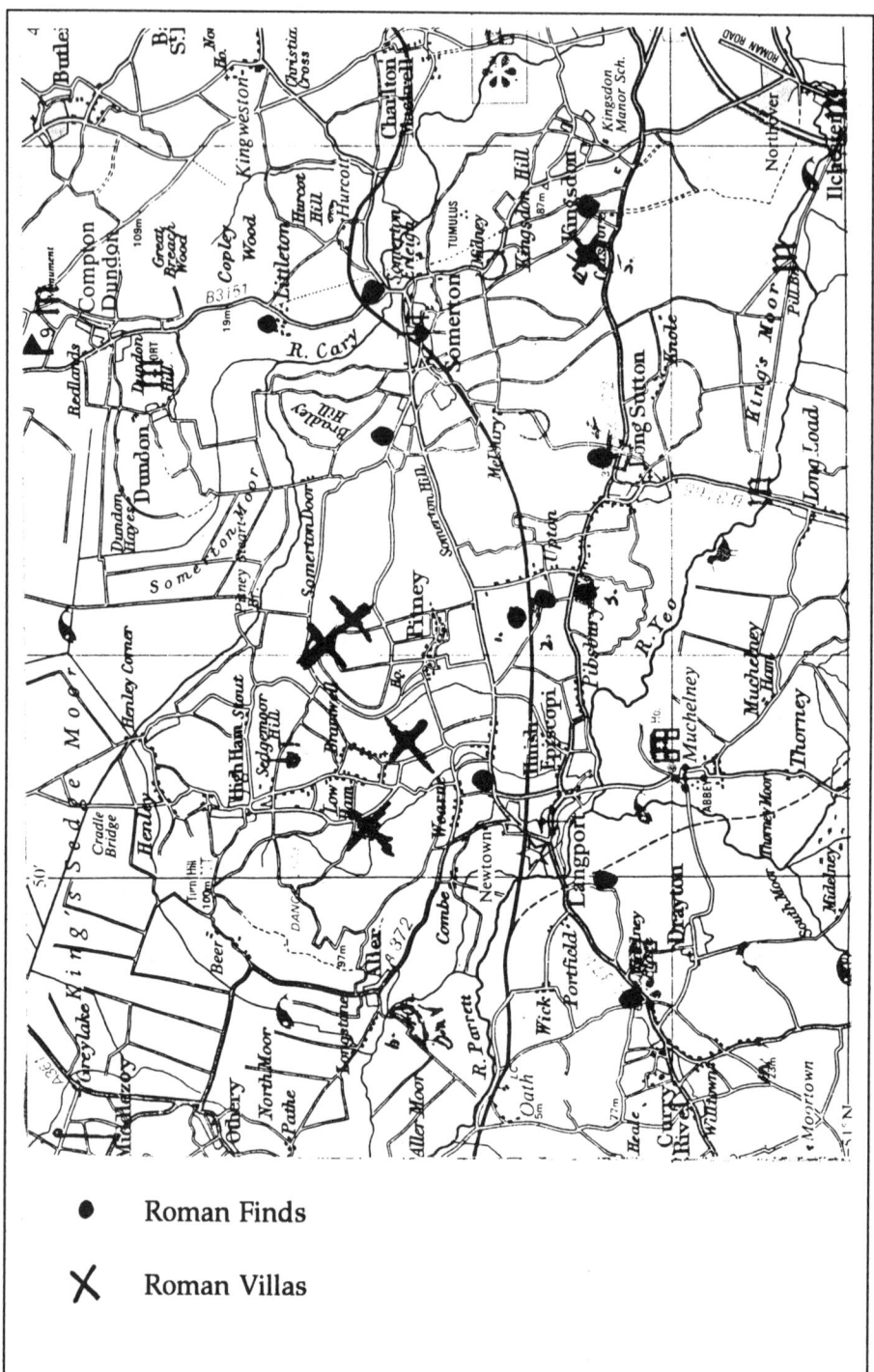

- ● Roman Finds
- ✗ Roman Villas

Above: The Loves of Dido and Aeneas as depicted in the Low Ham Mosaics.

Opposite: Map of Langport district indicating whereabouts of Roman villas and Roman finds.

overall an estimated six hundred were left behind. These, designed to give the occupants as much sunshine as possible, showed signs of a high degree of material prosperity.

The description by Sidonious, Bishop of Auvergne, who wrote about the time the Saxons were beginning their incursions on Roman Britain, exactly suits those buildings destroyed in the invasion. In some cases there had been direct transition from Celtic farm to Romano-British villa, as has been traced at Catsgore, near Somerton, where a round wooden hut was replaced by a mortared stone house.

Large country houses with great halls, libraries, baths and even tennis courts, were used as hunting lodges from where wealthy owners could chase the wolf and wild boar in the forests. There would have been a furnace room with an intricate system of pipes to supply warm and vapour baths. Water was brought via lead pipes or drawn from wells of excellent construction. The mosaic pavements of the villa were perfectly set in cement and supported on pillars of brick or stone. In the hollow space beneath, hot air could circulate, rising through flues in the walls which could be regulated by valves. The ladies' dining-room, the wool room, the store closets, the wainscotted main dining-room and the winter sitting-room all came into the Bishop's description.

It has been recorded that the lower portions of these villas were built of stone ,and the walls were of timber, then so plentiful in every district. Strong beams were necessary both to support upper storeys, for the Romans it is said disliked sleeping on the ground floor, and to bear the weight of the stone tiles on the roof. There were corn and oil stores, barns and granaries.

Outside fountains spouted water into stone basins from bronze spouts made in the form of lions' heads. There were trim hedges and long strips of lawn. Around the villa, whose walls were often covered with white plaster, were clustered the huts (the nucleus of hamlets or villages) of British labourers or slaves whose work would be directed by overseers also of the British race. Upper-class Britons were then widely divided from the lower class.

At the lower end of the scale was the two or three roomed rectangular house. The larger room, possibly the living area, may have been heated, while the smaller rooms could have been bedrooms or bed cupboards.

A wooden church may have been built in Langport at some time in these years. It is more likely to have been built in the peaceful and prosperous days of Roman rule then later in the troubled years of war after the Roman withdrawal.

Mention was made in 280AD by Tertullian of a centre of Christian conversion at Glastonbury as early as 166AD. It is said Joseph of Arimathea, or some others, built a little church of willows, preserved as a most ancient shrine long after the surrounding buildings were made of stone. Glastonbury is the one piece of English ground where Christianity once established, was never over-thrown. It has been recorded too that Huish Episcopi had its own withy church ... perhaps at a time Christianity was a persecuted creed in Rome. But authorities have written no indications as yet have been found to confirm there were ever Christians in Somerset during the Roman period.

Caesar had described the Britons as a race living on fleshmeat and dressed in skins. Later they became known even on the Continent for their corn and cloth. But when the Romans withdrew, comfort and culture went with them. Civilization was only skin deep – it wore off.

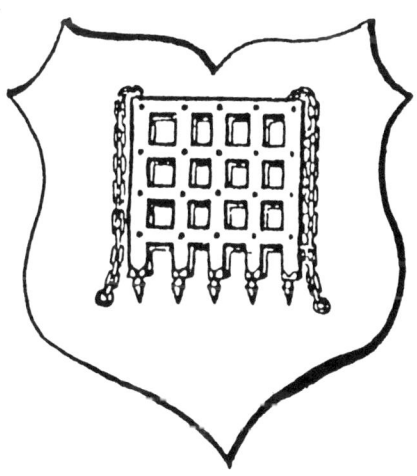

Langport Portcullis

Chapter 2

*Saxon Invasion of Somerset - Battle of Llongborth - Cerdic - Cenwalch -
Battle of Penselwood - Saxons in Langport - Centwine -
Ine and his laws - founding of Muchelney Abbey -
Langport part of Somerton royal manor, 500-800AD*

In 495AD the West Saxons, utterly hostile to Roman civilization, landed on the south coast. Being such a warlike people, they preferred fighting and taking what they wanted from others, to working their poor and badly cultivated lands in Germany. They lived the life of pirates, sailing from place to place in their warships, landing and carrying off corn and cattle at the point of the sword. The strength and daring of these 'English' Saxons, who gave the name England to the southern part of these islands – a tall, fine-looking race of men with golden hair and blue eyes – had long made them a terror to the inhabitants of the neighbouring coasts.

Somerset – the moors gave their name to the county, *i.e.* sea-moor settlers/*Somersetee* – was not the first point of attack by the Saxons. Its conquest had been delayed to some extent by the screen which the great Forest of Selwood presented in the east, ranging from Chippenham to the Dorset Downs at Cerne Abbas. The Forest was a large area of primeval woods, inhabited by bears, wild boars and packs of wolves. Dynastic quarrels, disputes and revolts of their own under-kings had also proved a great hindrance to the Saxon advance. Early Saxons were incapable of union, so we need not wonder too much why the war of conquest against the Britons dragged on for so long.

In our area, in both British and Saxon periods in history, the River Parrett has been the limit and boundary of advance for the invading foe, as well as a racial boundary. One of the early engagements fought between the two was the Battle of Llongborth, details of which, although not found in the *Anglo-Saxon Chronicle*, were recorded by Llywarch Hen, who has

Opposite: Alfred's Tower.

been mentioned already. His elegy was a lament for the death of Geraint, who had been fighting by his side in the battle, and who had been a prince of *Damnonia* (or *Dyvnaint*, or Devon).

It is said British forces were commanded by Arthur, Geraint's cousin, who too appears to have been a prince of Damnonia and an able leader in the wars. Legend takes the place of history in the story of 'King Arthur', who most probably represents the last leader of a British army using cavalry trained to the Roman pattern to hold off for a time the barbarian invaders when the Romans withdrew. His name is linked with Glastonbury and South Cadbury, but even after intensive investigation, no conclusive evidence has yet been found to prove his existence. Stories of his skill and courage in leading the last attempts to preserve the heritage of Rome in Britain show how strong an impact the Romans made on the Britons. Beyond this, Arthur remains a mythical figure – the enigmatic Arthur.

The fierce and bloody battle said to have been drawn, appears to have been against Saxon Cerdic, who founded the royal line of Wessex, probably about 530AD. In favour of the site being Langport, no other landing-place can be found whose name so closely resembles Llongborth. The position of Langport was on the very borders of Damnonia. The British appear to have had possession of the battlefield. The Saxons could easily have attacked by coming in their vessels up the Parrett, having sailed round to the Severn Sea as they had done in former years.

It the battle *was* an early attempt upon Somerset by the Parrett, we must believe that Cerdic then retired from the area although he had killed Geraint, for there was a pause of some years in the Saxon invasion before Cenwalch, son of Cynegils, entered mid-Somerset and 'drove the Britons as far as the Parrett' having defeated them at Penselwood, the densely forested area on the eastern boundary of the county, in 658AD. That victory opened the way through forests and marshes to the River Parrett – the clearing and settlement being a slow and gradual process.

During the lull, in 635AD Cynegils had been converted to Christianity so the war took on a different character. It was no longer the conquest of the Christian by the bloodthirsty heathen, but the subjugation of one Christian power to another. The *Anglo-Saxon Chronicle* relates what must have been a memorable event for the people of Langport, and all the inhabitants up to the line of the river, the new frontier of the West Saxons, with then half of Somerset under their jurisdiction. The town had a Saxon master and Saxons in its streets.

But the invaders no longer had the same desire to destroy as in years before. It was said of Cenwalch 'Those whom he conquered were his brethren – he came not, therefore, as Hengist (who led the first hordes) and Aella, simply to destroy'. His boundaries were enlarged, but the conquest no longer meant death or slavery to the conquered - it no longer meant the overthrow of the Christian faith. Cenwalch's own brother seems to have retired soon afterwards as a hermit to the wilds of Athelney, and there his noble character and 'prompt succor of all who sought his help' made him famous.

The Saxons, unlike the Romans, eventually brought in thousands of their countrymen as settlers who gave to the country a population with entirely new ideas and new customs. They preferred village life to that of the town. Families settled in hamlets, one or more making their home in each, preserving their own family existence independently of other families or villages. The tribe or clan of a hundred households formed the Hundred. Langport was placed in the Hundred of Somerton under a lord. The Saxon kept the wood or heath or fen jealously as a frontier around his village; whosoever crossed that space must proclaim his coming by horn, or run the risk of being cut down as an enemy.

At that time the country from the Parrett to Exmoor, fifty miles long by twenty miles wide, was a continuous forest abounding in game of all kinds, especially deer. We hardly realise how widespread were the forest lands. Even in the days of the Norman Conquest, twelve acres of woodland were mentioned at Muchelney. There was a wood at Somerton – another at Curry Rivel two miles long and a mile wide. Throughout the Saxon period, game, boar flesh and venison formed a major part of diet.

Cenwalch retained all the land from Somerton to the Parrett in his own hands as crown land, and probably kept up Langport's earthworks with great care, not daring to neglect them as long as the Damnonian Britons still held the entrenchments on Hurds Hill. He left the subject Britons to continue their trade and river traffic, under conditions of payment of royal dues to himself.

After Cenwalch's death, Wessex fell into dire disorder, and our own neighbourhood was deeply affected: Centwine (676-685AD), according to a poem by Adhelm, seems to have won three victories over the British finding they were meditating rebellion, and inflicted terrible slaughter on them. There was ceaseless war-fare in our area until all that was left was within Hurd's Hill earthworks, whose soil became sodden with the blood of Britons fighting a losing battle. With their iron-headed spears and two-edged swords, the Saxons were as pitiless as they were fearless. In 682AD Centwine drove the rebels as far as the sea. This seems to have been a great victory over the Damnonian Britons, but not the last.

After conquest came peaceful settlement. Centwine reigned prosperously for many years after the fighting. He built many new churches, retiring into a monastery at the close of his reign. In the early days of Saxon Christianity, retiring into the peace of the cloisters was not an infrequent act of great men, wearied with the burden of their rank.

King Ine's father, Cenred, was a direct descendant of Cerdic, whose centre had been Somerton. Ine's reign from 688AD was the next most important period, and his chief operations were against Devon and the West, i.e. Damnonia. In 710AD Ine defeated in a great battle the then British King Geraint, who reigned from the Parrett to Land's End – a not inconsiderable kingdom – and founded the town of Taunton. Langport had to contribute its quota of fighting men to the wars, according to the custom set out in Ine's laws. The attendance of men from every place was compulsory at the *fyrd*, or summoning of the host by the earldorman of the county, under penalty of fine to the half of his wergild or value of his person (*wer-man* and *gild* – gold).

It could be that the foundation of Muchelney Abbey in 933AD, was not only a thanksgiving by Ine for his victory over Geraint, but also further extension of his kingdom. He must often have passed along Langport's Bow Street as he travelled between his castles at Taunton and Somerton, or came to view the building of his Abbey, or be present at its hallowing, with his princes and other great men. Early charters confirm there had been a small monastic settlement in Muchelney dedicated to St. Peter and St. Paul about 750AD. Later this Abbey was destroyed by the Danes, only to be rebuilt by Athelstan in subsequent years.

Saxon kings gave large territories to the Church in spite of their constant wars, monasteries, which were manufacturing, agricultural and literary centres, were founded and respected. At Muchelney the monks drove rhines (drainage ditches) through the moors, and tilled the marsh lands. The missionary activities of the monks largely made up for the lack of district churches, their asceticism being a useful protest against the lusts and excesses of Saxon life. There was communication between churchmen in England and those on the continent. Arts and sciences were imported from abroad. The Church instructed men to become skilful in various handicrafts. Readers and thinkers were born out of people shortly before sunk in savagery and heathenism.

Ine's laws give glimpses of the life and manners of his age. Amidst his social legislation was an order that the ceorl's house should be fenced in winter and summer. In their open field system of co-operative farming, the rule was that individual portions of common pasture and arable land (such as Langport had in the moors) should also be fenced. Each holding consisted of a bundle of strips equal in quantity to the strips of other holdings. Anyone who neglected to fence his portion so that wild animals or cattle belonging to the community strayed in, was held responsible for any damage done. Probably it was the work of the whole community to reclaim land from river and forest, and to cultivate it in common as partners.

King Ina's Palace.

The laws show traces of payment of rent from the cultivators – paid in kind when the lord visited the land. Langport, as part of Somerton royal manor, would have had to help feed the king and his court at stated times when they passed to hunt, or on a journey, or to war. From an estate of ten hides, say 1200 acres, the lord could claim 300 loaves, 10 vessels of honey, 42 ambers of ale, 2 oxen, 10 rams, 10 geese, 20 hens, 10 cheeses, 100 eels, 5 salmon and 20pounds of fodder. Money compensation for murder was settled according to the rank of the injured person, *viz.* twice as much for the noble as for the squire (*thane*), and twice as much for the squire as for the yeoman (*ceorl, churl*). The Saxon *churl* had a *wergild* of 200 shillings, but the British/Welsh *churl* was only rated at 120 shillings, showing the lower value set on the conquered race. Squires, companions and attendants on the King, were priced at 1200 shillings, and the noble (*earldorman*) or bishop at 4800 shillings. For other serious crimes, a man had to find a certain number of friends possessed of so many hides of land to swear to his innocence – the swearing power of each man like his *wergild* again depending on this rank and/or property.

Ine did much for Somerset. His efforts were successfully directed towards welding together the two races of Briton and Saxon into one people. It was his deliberate policy to deal with his British subjects amicably, and to give them political rights along with the Saxons. King Ine resigned his crown after a reign of thirty-seven years, and went on a pilgrimage to Rome where he ended his days.

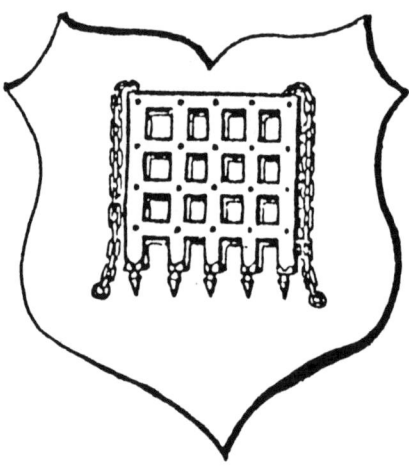

Chapter 3

The arrival of the Danes - year of nine Battles - King Alfred - Danegeld - Athelney - Battle of Ethandune - Baptism of Guthrum - Treaty of Wedmore - Danelaw.

As the Saxons had dealt with the Britons, so the Danes dealt with the Saxons. The endless wars between Saxon and Briton, or between one Saxon kingdom and another, which had continued for nearly four hundred years, were succeeded by deadly struggles between Saxon and Dane for another two hundred years from the close of the eighth century. The chief kingdoms were Northumbria in the North: Mercia in the Midlands, East Anglia, Kent, Sussex and Essex in the East, and Wessex (the most advanced in religion, learning and all we call civilization) in the South and South-West.

When the first three Viking ships from Norway and Denmark landed on the south coast in 787AD, the local reeve (town representative) attempted getting payment from them, then driving them on to Dorchester. But those strangers were not sheep to be sheared for the benefit of the King. They were fierce war wolves, who seemed to have an absolute thirst for blood and a savage pleasure in destruction. Of all the fierce fighting men of the time, the Danes were the fiercest, and they invaded in hundreds – some say thousands. Records of their harrying, of devastation by fire and sword, of wild lawlessness and contempt for human life, are repeated one page after another in the *Anglo-Saxon Chronicle*.

They did have some noble qualities. It required the Danish wars to purify Saxon manhood and teach the petty kingdoms the lesson of unity. Continual striving between one kingdom and another had left the Saxons in such a state of exhaustion, they were too weak and jealous of one another to combine against a new common enemy. The reeve was slaughtered in that encounter, yet no effort appears to have been made to avenge his death, or even to find shipping to guard the coast. The art of seamanship appeared to have been lost to the Saxons, who not only had forgotten their old pirate habits by which means in earlier days their forefathers had overcome our island, but even how to build ships!

Built for speed, Danish long-ships with their dark sails, holding one or two hundred men or more, could find their way up the most shallow of rivers. The treacherous 'Gore Sands' at the mouth of the Parrett would have held no fears for these marauders when they attacked there in 845AD. To sail up and down the tidal river on the 'bore', only an hour or two from Langport's bridge, would have been simple. When there was no tide, the ships were towed for miles.

Viking ship.

At Uphill, close to the mouth of the river Axe, a story is told how Wessex men overcame and destroyed the Danes because a certain old woman, too lame to run when her village was burnt and robbed, dared to cut the ropes of the enemy's ships during the fight inland, setting them adrift on the ebbing tide. The Danes were unable to save themselves. They could not get back to their bases in the Severn Sea, the two islands Steep Holm and Flat Holm. This is the first record in the *Anglo-Saxon Chronicle* of the Danes in the Severn Sea. The British of South Wales, still bitter enemies of the Saxons (the distinction between Bret/Welsh and Saxon being clearly defined in Ine's laws as we know) received the Danes in their harbours, enabling them to cross constantly, plundering the Somerset coast.

Two-thirds of England was in the enemy's hands by the year 871AD. Only Wessex was left. That was the year of a great organised attack on our area by the Danes. That was the year of battles – nine in all – and that was the year when Alfred, twenty-two years old, the recognised heir, succeeded to the throne of Wessex, when his brother King Aethelred was killed in conflict. On Alfred, that great King, fell the burden of fighting the Danes, and he rolled back the tide of heathen conquest from his land. Alfred's heroism was not only that of a patriot enduring every extremity in resisting the invaders of his country. he was a champion of Christ against the savage heathen whom, when he had the mastery, he won over to his own faith. As a sovereign of failing health and by temperament a scholar, he had many-sided talents. He created a fleet. He built ships of sixty oars or more to resist the pirates from overseas. He set up a sound and just administration worked through the shire and its officers. It was all very primitive but better than anything there had been before in England. If ever the men of Langport were to have their share in great events, this was the time.

Alfred paid gold to the Danes to secure peace and gain time after those nine terrible battles. Money well spent, as peace was kept for four years. The Danes wintered in London, then part of Mercia, well outside the boundaries of Alfred who obtained a welcome respite. The enemy went north into Northumbria, Lincolnshire, the Midlands, and everywhere were victorious. In 876AD the truce ended. Alfred found it necessary to make a second peace the following year, purchased again with gold.

That Easter, a force under Danish Ubbe landing at an unknown spot – possibly Combwich – and drove Saxon Odda into a stronghold. The latter sallied forth, it is said, defeated the Danes and he himself slew Ubbe. Cannington Park might well have sheltered the Saxons and the ground below have been the site of the battle, for in Cannington Park quarry great trenches full of skeletons were discovered – an estimated thousand – many with signs of having met with a violent death.

Early in 878AD, when mid-winter held the Wessex men in imaginary security, with the cutting-off of communications, the isolation of villages, and the great difficulty of doing anything, the Danes swooped and made themselves masters of the county. Concerning details of that dreadful winter we have few. It was a time of ravaged farms, burnt villages, razed churches and monasteries, and sacked towns. To the Danes themselves, the conquest must have seemed complete. The King had disappeared.

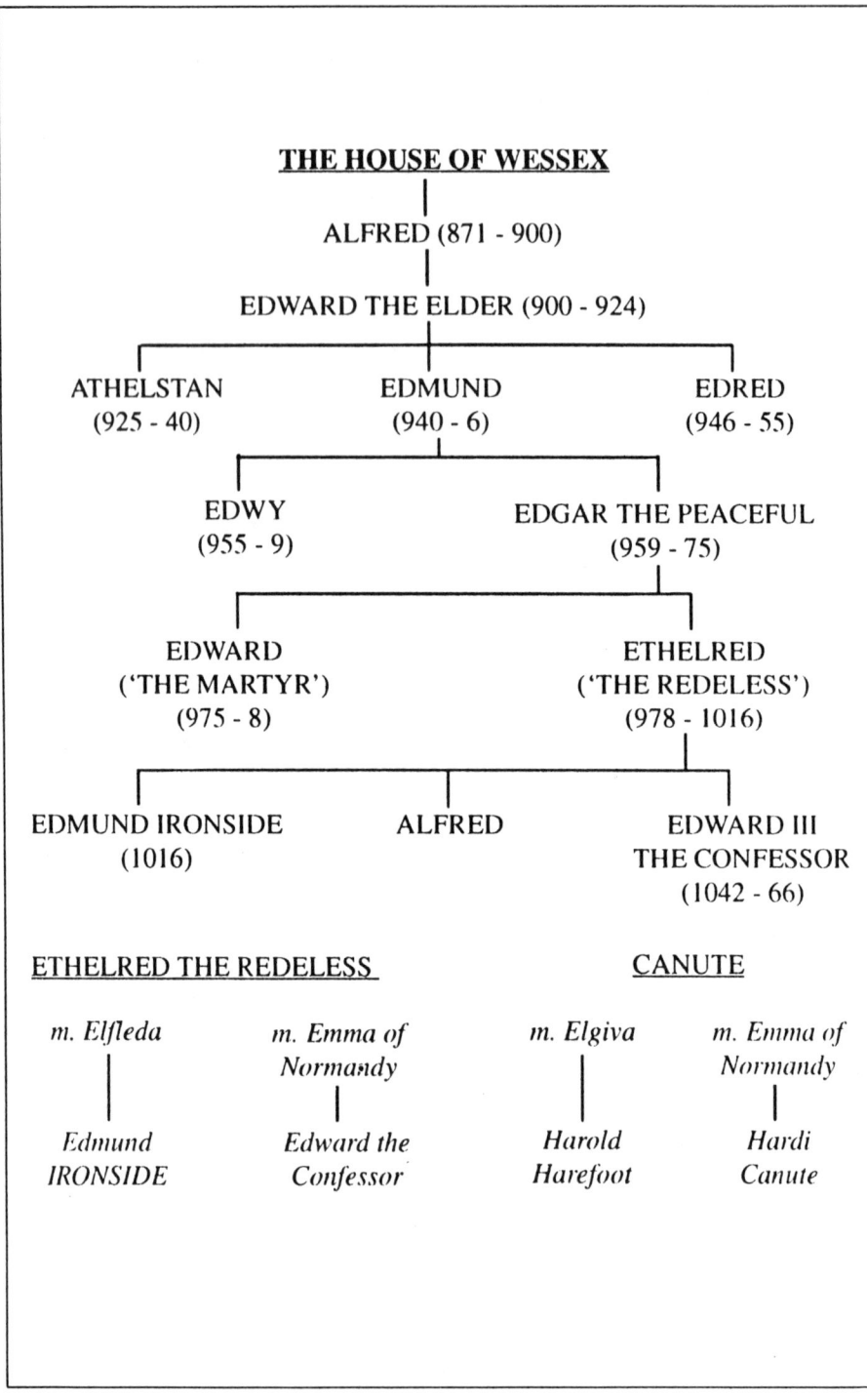

There was no longer any army in the field.

Alfred escaped with his family and nobles into the swamps and moors of our neighbourhood at Athelney. Bishop Asser, his biographer, described the place as an island 'surrounded on all sides by water, and by vast impassable peat bogs. Access can be had to it only by causeways, or by a single bridge built and lengthened out with great labour between two elevated forts. Towards the Western extremity of the bridge a fort of very great strength and most beautiful construction has been raised by the King.'

In Athelney Alfred and his followers were able to live by hunting and fishing, and safe from pursuit, could send out messengers to learn what was going on outside their hiding place. Alfred may have gone about disguised to encourage the report of his death or flight from the land. One tale told is he took his harp and in the role of a glee-man (wandering minstrel), went to the Danish camp at Chippenham. Unsuspected, he amused the enemy so well with song and music, he was able to remain for several days, planning for the Spring.

Alfred renewed the entrenchments on the Eastover and Westover hills in Langport. He provided for the maintenance of its bridges. In Athelney he held the Danes at bay making frequent sorties on them, harassing their supplies, while secretly assembling large forces from those men of Somerset, Wilts and Hants. who had not fled the country as so many had done. The enemy acted with no less caution.

Danish King, Guthrum, who had wintered with his army at Chippenham, summoned Danes who had settled elsewhere in England to add to his forces, for he saw there was danger in delay as local opposition and activity increased daily. The renewal of hostilities was not altogether the work of Alfred, for had he not been backed by the tenacity, and the obstinacy of a people who knew not when they were beaten, he would have effected nothing. He could depend upon no other help than that of the men of Somerset, a folk of the forest and moors, a fisher folk, a rough wild people, who were not daunted by the superior numbers of the enemy, nor by the terror of their name, nor by their victorious invasion of the whole country. When the new army of Alfred was at last brought together behind the protection of Selwood Forest, he went to head them and the *Anglo-Saxon Chronicle* tells how over-joyed the people were to see their young King alive and well amongst them. He led them on to fight one of the most decisive battles of the world's history in 878AD, saving England and Europe from heathen conquest.

Bratton Castle, a fort at Dunball, is said to have been the entrenchment of the Danes. The Battle of Ethandune, near Edington in Wiltshire, began at noon, lasting for several hours. The cries of the combatants could be heard for miles around. After a fourteen-day siege, the Danes surrendered. All who had not taken refuge in the fort were killed. Their cattle and everything with them were seized by the Saxons. The Danes had often been beaten in battle (victory or defeat could be uncertain). It was the end they looked to. If they could renew their struggle, they cared little for a setback, but this time they were desperate. They had no provisions, and allowed Alfred to dictate such terms as they had never before been forced to accept. Guthrum promised to receive baptism under Alfred and become a Christian. 'All of which things (says Asser) Guthrum performed according to promise.'

Florence of Worcester says of the Baptism itself 'Guthrum, the King of the Pagans came with thirty of his principal warriors to King Alfred at a place called Aller near Athelney, and there the King received him as his son by adoption, raised him up from the font of holy baptism and gave him the name of 'Athelstan.' Aller Church stood on an island, and then was not only surrounded by fens, but also by woods of alder, which have now disappeared. The woods would have hidden the village from the Danes, and the waters would have been a natural moat around it, offering a refuge to Langport, Muchelney, Somerton and other places previously ravaged by the enemy.

There were seven weeks of instruction before Guthrum was brought to baptism. His conversion was the first step to the Christianising of the fierce Danes. Thereafter, a new element of strength and energy was added to the nation. A new unity grew out of the upheavals of the Danish conquests. As long as the Viking battle-axe was crashing through the skulls of monks, and the English were nailing to their church-doors skins flayed off their Danish enemies, the hatred between the two was complete. But it was not permanent. After the Danes had accepted baptism, it was easy to merge them with the English under the rule of the House of Wessex for they had not come to found a Scandinavian Empire. They had come to seek good farmlands. Settled down prosperously in their new quarters, under their own Danish laws and Danish earls and lawmen,

Opposite below: Burrow Mump.

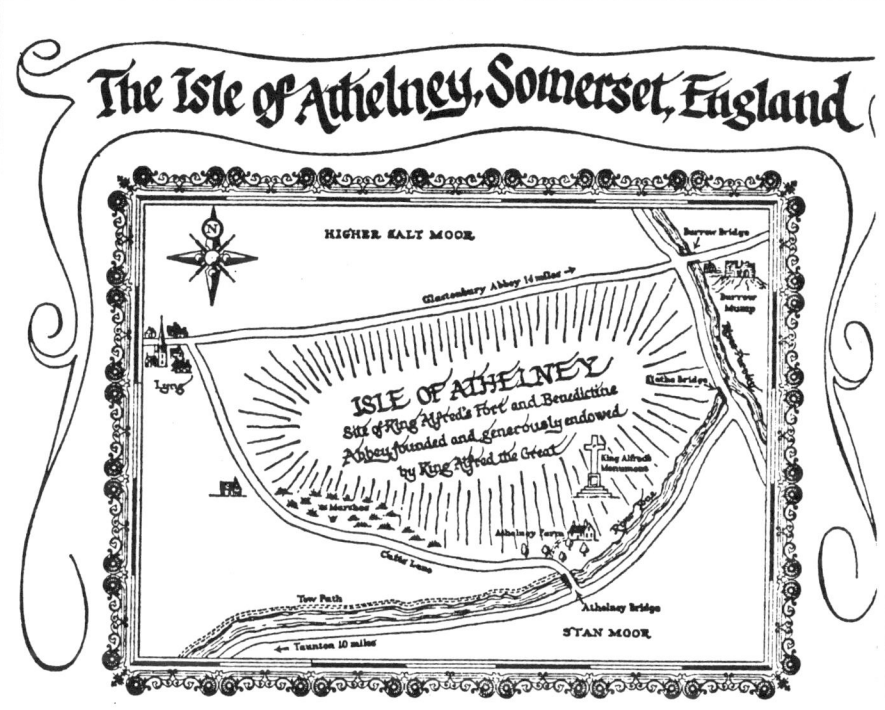

they could tolerate the light rule of English Kings. By the Treaty of Wedmore, Guthrum and Alfred divided England between them at the line of Watling Street. Guthrum's part became known as the Danelaw.

This was not a final settlement between Dane and Saxon, but it was a temporary measure of relief. For a time the land had peace. Alfred founded a monastery on the island of Athelney about 888AD, as a thank-offering for his victory, but found it difficult to obtain men of devotion and learning to occupy it. Christianity and culture had all but disappeared in the wars. Abbeys and churches were charred ruins. 'Throughout all England everything was harried and burnt,' said Alfred. The King, therefore, sent to Wales and to the continent for clergy and teachers. John the Saxon was made Abbot of Athelney. Records show in 1534 there was an Abbot and twelve monks. It was dissolved in 1539.

In 1693, about four miles away at North Newton, an Anglo-Saxon jewel, now in the Ashmolean Museum, Oxford, was found depicting a nobleman carrying two flowers. The jewel, of coloured enamel and set in gold, bore a border inscribed:

AELFRED MEC HEHT GEWYRCAN
[Alfred ordered me to be made]

Possibly at one time this was held in Alfred's Abbey, for it may have been the end of a pointer used for the study of an important book. Pointers accompanied each copy of the King's translation of Pope Gregory's "Pastoral Care", sent to every diocese in his kingdom. The work was intended to play an important part in encouraging young men to learn English. Those destined for the church studied Latin. Or some say the jewel may have been set in Alfred's iron helmet, on which he wore his crown, and from which it could have been lost.

There was a second great storm of Danish invasion in 892 AD. Probably Langport men were again in the Somerset defence forces, for we are told that the boroughs did good service in the wars. At Alfred's death at the end of the eighth century, his son, Edward the Elder, carried the struggle on unceasingly.

We are inclined to attribute our own folk song of the 'Black Dog of Langport' to those times. The black dog was a common form in which the devil was supposed to show himself, according to folklore, with whom the heathen pagan was said to have been in league:

The Black Dog o' Langport have a burned off his tail
And this is the night of our jolly wassail:
vor 'tis our wassail And 'tis your wassail,
And joy be you, vor 'tis our wassail.
Wassail, wassail, all over the town,
Your cup it is white and your beer it is brown,
Your bowl it is made of the good ashen tree,
And your beer it is brewed of the best barley,
Langport bull dog have lost his big tail
In the night that we go singing wassail.

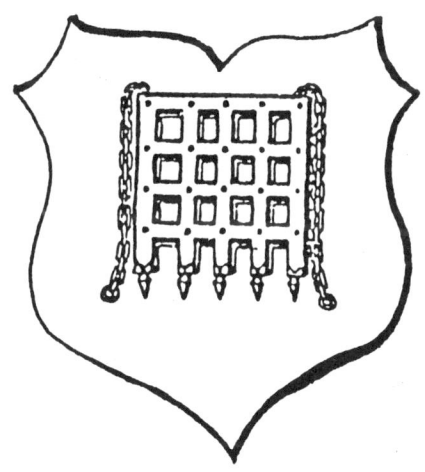

Chapter 4

Burghal Hidage 912 A.D. - Langport as a borough (burh) - agricultural system - trade - market - Edward the Elder - Athelstan (925-940AD) - Rebuilding of Muchelney Abbey - Langport granted a mint.

The oldest existing document in which Langport Borough is mentioned is the 'Burghal Hidage' dated about 912AD, being a survey of military organisations arranged to withstand the influx of the Danes. In the 'Hidage' Langport Borough (*burh*), created by Alfred, had 600 hides assigned to it, one hide being reckoned as 120 acres. Langport was the centre of a large district requisitioned to maintain the entrenchments and palisades (according to records 2475 feet of walls), and provide all the services required to keep an efficient stronghold, in which neighbouring people were to take refuge in case of attack.

In those Anglo-Saxon times, it was laid down as a rule of law that 'every man must have a lord', who was bound to fight for his King by bonds of loyalty. Each lord devoted his life to hunting and war, and to the service of his own overlord, the King, or to some greater lord than himself, or a Bishop or Abbot, and to satisfy the King's requirement he kept houses in the 'burhs' and burgesses in those houses.

Langport's burgesses, whose lack of real military training led them to be considered despicable in a fighting age, were yet kept in the 'burh' for military purposes, fed by the manor to which they belonged. They were usually a great man's retainers, ready to contribute their share towards the three pressing national requirements, the 'trinoda necessitas', from which no *thegn* (thane) nor *churl* (ceorl) might ever free himself, *viz.*

1) the *fyrd-fare*, or going forth with the host (army)
2) the *burh bote* or maintenance of the *burh* entrenchments, and
3) the *bridge bote* or duty of keeping up the bridges.

Burgesses, not sharers in the town lands, thought themselves superior to the villagers, but men of knightly rank considered them low class. They had a precarious worldly position. At any time they could lose all their wealth through fire, borough houses being of wood. Generally, they were considered vulgar, only keen on making money.

The *churl*, another important member of the borough, was a freeman who had police powers in his own house, and who had to be compensated if anyone invaded his dwelling or broke through his hedge. He who 'throve to thegn right' was described as having five hides (six hundred acres) of his own land, and a bell tower, as well as a house in the street of the borough, if he wished to rise in the world and keep retainers to help maintain the stone walls, store provisions, and fight behind the fortifications if necessary.

The largest towns did not include more than seven or eight thousand people. Langport had less than three hundred inhabitants by the time of the *Domesday Book*, which would include people from outside villages ruled by different lords – not only those bound by proprietary or agricultural ties. The commercial element in the town became uppermost in the century before Domesday, and houses which should have been occupied by burgesses or churls, became occupied by tradesmen.

Langport men grew rich by means of their sheep and cattle grazing in the moors, by their markets, and by the tillage of the 'Town Field' (near Bond's Pool). The scarce and highly valued meadows were allocated under strict rules of proportionate division by the community. The burgesses had to agree to the same rules for the rotation and cultivation of crops, and after harvest, the strips returned to the state of an open field in common use. This was the main system of agriculture to around 1500AD. The right of using the common moors, the number and kind of animals pastured in them, hedges and drainage were regulated by the community. Reeves of the moors were elected by the town, ordered the impounding of animals that trespassed, and managed the drainage and police duties of the moors. The *hayward* had to set up hedges, and remove them for arable and pasture purposes. He too was elected by the community. The reclaiming of land from the waste of the moors, embanking of rivers, or the cutting down of woods was allowed by the lord of the manor to the free tenants, provided sufficient pasture was left as common. The lord of Langport granted some rights of common, and the Corporation granted other rights to burgesses down to the nineteenth century. The people, be

Above: Muchelney Church ceiling;
Opposite above: Muchelney Abbey;
Opposite below: The Priest's House.

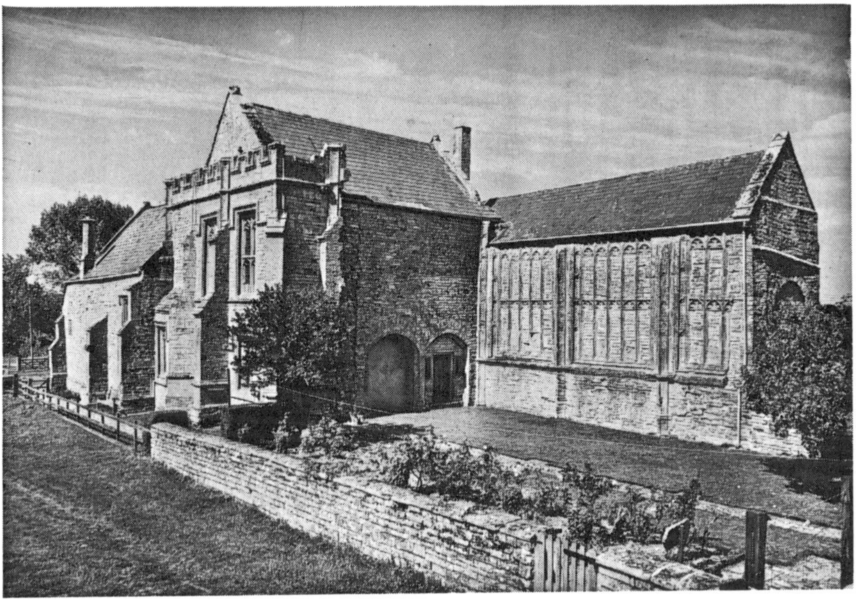

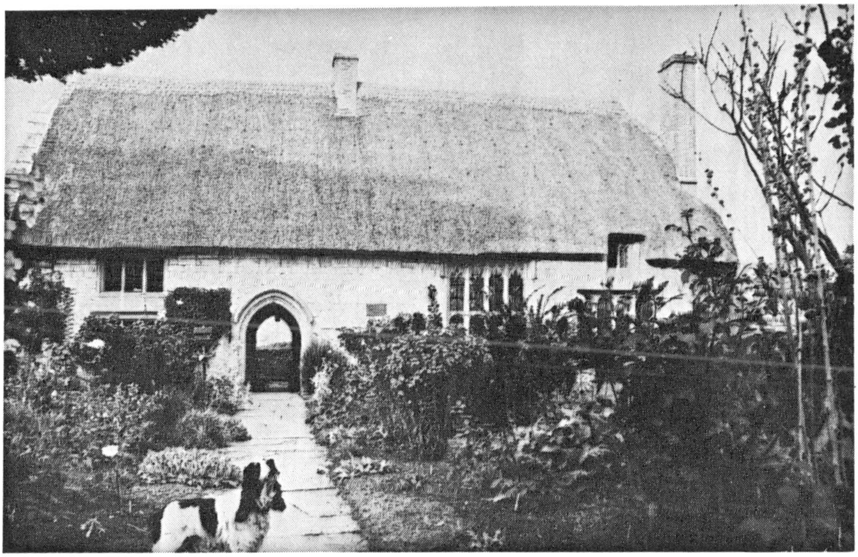

they lord, thegns, or free tenants, were shareholders in the land of the borough, the share varying as a whole share (a hide), a half share (half-hide), or a quarter (vergate), a half-vergate (the extent of land an ox could plough in a year, which varied from 8 to 24 acres), or a quarter vergate (farthing).

Trade was to be found in weekly markets where surplus produce was sold from booths: the market paying tolls to the portreeve, from whom the traders required a licence. From Edward the Elder to William I, King after King legislated against trading outside the borough, not only because these places were fortified, but because here could be found a permanent official like the portreeve, the most ancient officer of the town, to supervise. It was his job to act for the town with the King: to collect taxes and food rents: raise levies of fighting men: manage local police matters, and act as coroner or elect the coroner and constables, or their equivalent. He may also have served as steward under the lord, as the role of steward or bailiff was only distinguished from that of the portreeve in later times.

Edward the Elder, Alfred's son (900-924 AD), with his sister Ethelfleda of Mercia (as brave as himself) won back from the Danes most of the country Alfred had agreed to give them. No English King until the reign of Edward had been as powerful, for he had all England as far as the Humber under his own rule. Somerset, being dear to Alfred, who could never forget the great crisis of his life passed in Athelney, had been bestowed upon Edward by his father. Edward, it has been supposed, gave to the bishopric of Wells, the manor of Huish Episcopi, which may explain why the village of Huish has always held the mother church of the parish, and the Borough of Langport until the late nineteenth century, has had the daughter church as a chapelry subordinate to the parish of Huish.

Athelstan succeeded his father in 925AD and reigned for fifteen years. As a child, he had been close to Alfred, who gave him a jewelled belt and gold-hilted sword, and dressed him in the purple cloak of a royal knight. Nor was Alfred disappointed in the hopes he formed of his grandson, who proved himself a great general. Men told too of his learning, and of his pious devotion to the Church of England, on which he showered gifts with a lavish hand.

Some dispute is said to have arisen about Athelstan's right to the throne. A story is preserved (not proven) that on learning one of his brothers was plotting against him, he caused the brother to be put to sea in an open boat with only one attendant. The prince, in despair, jumped overboard and was drowned, but his companion with much difficulty was able to recover the prince's body and bring it back to shore. Plots against Athelstan were supposed to be based upon some defect of his birth, his mother being of servile origin. Whatever the truth, William of Malmesbury, the historian who recorded this story of the King, did so at least a hundred and fifty years after his death. But there is no doubt of Athelstan's visits to Langport or of his re-founding of Muchelney Abbey. In those years the King may have seen in Langport's weekly market, skins, wool and corn, side by side with sheep, oxen and swine. There would have been cheeses made from the milk of sheep and cows, barley bread and oat cakes, wild fowl and crates of fish, as well as salt and honey, and iron for agricultural implements. Honey was important since it took the place of sugar, and was used to make strong mead. Great use was made of salt, too, the cattle being killed and salted down, since it was impossible to feed them under shelter through the winter. As a rule, the luxuries, which the rich only could purchase at the great fairs as that of Winchester, could also be obtained from the travelling chapman, who brought furs, silks, gems, and articles of gold, silver and ivory with him on his visits.

Langport was as keen for trade as it was for fighting, as was seen by the early grant of a mint obtained in King Athelstan's reign, and which proved the importance the town had attained by his time. Langport was the trade centre of the Royal Manor of Somerton. Silver pennies from Langport's mint, which bore for the first time the historical fact that the King was 'King of all Britain' were the only coins in general use from the 8th century to 1350. If a man wanted a smaller coin, he broke the penny into halves and quarters. The penny would buy sufficient wheat to make bread for eight men, or fodder for five horses, when four pence was the price of a sheep. Minting was done under close supervision. It was a primary law 'let no man mint, save within port' (*porta*, gate) on pain of death.' The water under Little Bow Bridge was called 'Portlake', so probably the lower town gate and the mint were then in that area. The portreeve was answerable to the King for maintaining the standard and weight of the coin. The moneyer required a licence from the King, who received the profits of the coining and who exacted severe penalties for any form of false coinage. The moneyer knew that if he cheated, his handiwork could come to a swift conclusion, for men would see his hands nailed up outside his door as Athelstan ordained.

In addition to the moneyers (two under Athelstan being apparently men of war, Wynsige, the winner of victory, and Byrthelm, wearing a bright helmet), we might add as tradesmen of that day, the smith, baker, brewer, furrier, miller, and bowyer. Possibly slaves were to be found for sale in Langport market, for the portreeve was able to demand a toll of four pence on the sale of each. The treatment of slaves, found on every manor, was one of the worst characteristics of our early forefathers. They had no protection from master or mistress who had power of life and limb over them. They were tortured or loaded with chains for the slightest of offences, and were sold out of the land. Athelstan gave them a new rank in the realm by extending to them the same system of mutual insurance against crime, which was customary amongst freemen.

We are told how Athelstan went in royal progress from manor to manor. The King's court was a moving body, a little army eating its way from one royal estate to another, but with no home. The King's forerunners arrived ahead of the train at the spot destined for the King's visit, tapping the beer barrels, slaying and cooking the cattle, and baking the bread. Soon the long company came pounding in through the muddy roads, horsemen and spearmen, thegn and noble, bishop and clerk, the string of mules, the big waggons with the royal hoard and the royal wardrobe, and last of all the heavy standard borne by the King himself. Then followed the rough court of justice, for the King personally supervised the order of his kingdom, giving aid to the local courts (often helpless before the great lords), or punishing the reeves who had not fulfilled their duties correctly. Later came the huge banquet, which lasted into the night when the fires died down.

King Athelstan obtained from the Welsh princes as many dogs as he could for hunting, and trained falcons and hawks. The moors around Langport were for centuries famous for their wild fowl, giving the King every opportunity to indulge his love of hawking.

Men knew when their King would be among them; each manor and each town knew when to make their customary payments in kind; and all men knew when and where to make their cases, their pleas and gifts. As England became more consolidated, the royal progresses grew regular and methodical.

No Wessex King proved greater in his exploits at home, in the extent of his power, or in his influence abroad. By successful campaigns, he subdued the Welsh in Wales and Cornwall, so we heard no more of their risings. He married his four sisters to the chief princes in Europe, and in this way wove a web of alliances round the hostile Dane. He fostered commerce, and organised justice in the land furthering the civil and religious liberties of the people.

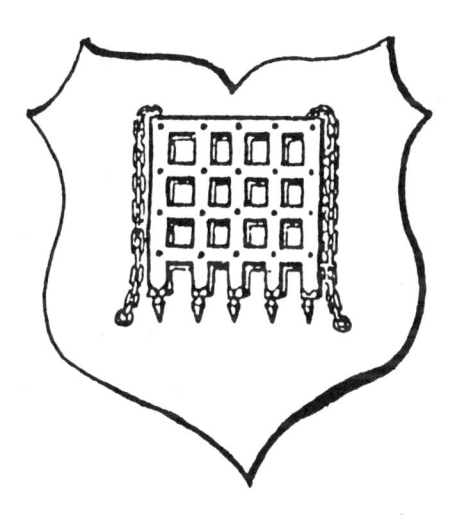

Chapter 5

'Frankpledge' - Church's influence - life of parish priest - Royal Hall in Langport - Langport's ancient Court - Hundred System - Ethelred the Unready (979-1017 A.D.) - recommencement of Danish wars. 940-1066 A.D.

After the early Danish wars, the state required *Frankpledge* as part of the base of social order, by which system each man was answerable for the life and conduct of others. An individual was enrolled in a company of ten neighbours. If one of the ten committed an injury and bolted, the remaining nine had to make amends for him. An elaborate system of fines provided for the valuation of each part of the person – one shilling for an injured fingernail – and each man had his price, or *wergild*. Robbery, perjury and plunder, evasion of market and city gate tolls were very frequent. Langport would have needed stocks and chains, prison house, and may have possessed a gallows on which to hang thieves and other offenders.

The Church was a very great and far-reaching influence on national life. We know that severe penances were imposed by the Saxon Church and accepted by the kings. From the cradle to the grave it forced on parishioners new laws of conduct, new habits, and new ideas of life and society. It entered the home, and limited the husband's power over wife, child and slave, proclaiming slavery an evil. The little Saxon Church on the Hill would have been the very centre of Langport.

Picture the life of the parish priest. Seven times a day he rang the church bell to call people to prayers. The service comprised the *Paternoster, Te Deum,* and the *Magnificat* chanted very slowly. Ecclesiastical laws insisted that 'if anyone sings out of tune or goes too quickly, he shall be turned out of church' and '... no-one is to bring hawks or pigs to church with him.' No man went to war without confessing his sins and receiving Holy Communion. At the church door banns were proclaimed and the slave made free, his freedom being recorded in the margin of the book of the Gospels.

The priest preached diligently on Sundays. Baptism could not be delayed beyond the thirty-seventh night, and all had to be confirmed. He taught the children handicrafts, as well as Christianity, reporting to the Bishop and mentioning anyone who had fallen into mortal sin. He instructed the people to avoid drunkenness, to give up heathenish songs and diabolical sports. He discouraged witchcraft. The worship of fountains, trees and stones was forbidden. The priest himself was warned against overdrinking and games of chance, and was forbidden to join in hunting and hawking, and instead was '... to divert himself with a book.' The unity of the Church in those days thus helped teach the many kingdoms to become a whole.

We assume there must have been a Royal Hall in Langport, which would have consisted of one lofty room with no upper room and no side rooms. If the lower wall was of stone, the upper parts would be built of wood, with wooden windows. There was often in the Saxon Hall a portico open in front, containing the lord's seat, and perhaps a tesselated floor. Benches would have been arranged all around, and in the upper part of the hall would have been a dais with a chair or throne for the King. The chamberlain would see that the servants decked the hall with courtly hangings and with weapons and trophies of the chase, and would issue the gold drinking cup from the luggage for the King's table. The King could be approached easily. The doors of the Hall were usually left open. Guests could come in and sit at his table unquestioned. The Portreeve and chief men of Langport would have had no difficulty in gaining admission into Athelstan's presence.

Besides being firstly, a fortification; and secondly a market, Langport also developed a *moot* or Court from the time of Athelstan, and these three constituents made an important line between Langport Borough and the ordinary town. A monthly Court would have been held under the Portreeve in Langport, the trade centre for a district of six Hundreds. The cattle thief would have been judged before this Court and the times being so rough, fines were inflicted on those who brawled at meetings. Theft and killings were common, with private warfare everywhere. Rogues took advantage of Danish plunderings to annex their neighbour's property. All the King could do was to try to confine such troubles within narrower limits. When the cattle thief was caught, he paid half the fine to the owner of the cattle, and the rest was divided between the lord and the Hundred.

Today Langport's ancient Court: 'The Court Leet and Court Baron, or

Customary Court of the Langport Town Trustees, Lords of the Manor of Langport Eastover.' meets only occasionally when there are fundamental changes relating to the Manor, which was created after the Norman Conquest, when every community had to continue to maintain peace and order in its own way and within its own boundaries.

The powers of this Court are such that decisions relating to the Manor, as long as they do not concern private property, are supreme and cannot be countermanded by any other Court in the land, or even by the Queen herself. The area over which today's Court has jurisdiction is small – being about fifty acres of moorland – Langport's Manor. The Court is still presided over by the Steward of the Manor of Langport Eastover, and two moor reeves, and the rights on the land are possessed by the commoners, who sell their rights each year by auction to farmers, who graze their cattle and horses thereon. Langport Manor is one of probably about six in the country, whose commoners have continued to meet every year since the Norman Conquest to discuss the maintenance of the moors, and elect moor reeves.

Under King Edgar (959-97 AD), Edward the Elder's grandson, Wessex reached its zenith. Edgar's reign was mainly remembered for his choice of St. Dunstan, his life-long friend, as chief advisor. Born near Glastonbury, the son of a wealthy thegn, Dunstan had been made Abbot of that town by King Edmund when scarcely twenty-years-old, and undoubtedly had much to do with the prosperity of the reign. Edgar ruled so wisely and well, he gained the title 'The Peaceable.' As an example, instead of taking tribute from the men of Wales, he asked for the heads of five hundred wolves yearly, so that the country might rid itself of these dangerous animals.

Edgar visited every part of his realm accompanied by Dunstan (made Archbishop of Canterbury in 960 AD), meeting his nobles and principal men of the country. Unhappily the period following his death marked the decay of Wessex royal power, which the King had not kept entirely in his own hands. The kingdom had been divided into earldoms, an earl ruling over each in the King's name. Hence the King's real authority was weakened, and before many more years were to pass, the Danes were able finally to conquer the whole land.

When Edgar died, his eldest son, Edward, was only fourteen or fifteen-years-old. Edward's own mother was dead and (we are told) his stepmother, Elfrida, wanted her own son Ethelred to be King instead. One day when Edward was out hunting, he left his companions and rode to Corfe Castle where his stepmother was living, to visit his little brother. On leaving and on his horse, he asked for a drink of wine. While drinking it, the heartless queen seized her opportunity and ordered one of her attendants to stab Edward in the back. The poor King at once put spurs to his horse and rode away. Before long he fainted, and falling from his animal, was dragged some way with his foot in the stirrups. When at last found by his companions, he was quite dead. This unfortunate young King is known as Edward the Martyr. He died after reigning only four years, and then the crown did go to his half brother, Ethelred.

So after fifty years cessation, Danish inroads re-commenced. Under Sweyn Forkbeard, King of Denmark, the Danes once more made South England the special object of their attack. The unity of Saxon and Dane in the island was still incomplete, and the weakness of the Kingdom under the foolish Ethelred – one of the most incompetent Kings that ever vexed the land (978-1016AD) – stood revealed. The Danes marched wherever they pleased, harrying, burning and murdering. The *Anglo-Saxon Chronicle* says '... there was so much awe of the host that no man could think how men could drive them from the earth, or hold this earth against them.' Every *shire* (earldom) of Wessex was devastated. The cowardly King continuously paid the Danes to keep away, without every trying to get his men together to fight, so of course they came again and again asking for a larger sum each time.

The exactions of Danish tribute were a terrible drain upon the people's possessions: those in surrounding districts would come into Langport from time to time to give up their silver and their jewels to be coined into money at the mint, as did the townspeople themselves. Churches and monasteries were stripped once more of their holy things. A record of these miseries is preserved by the coins now found in Stockholm and Copenhagen. *Danegeld* had been levied and paid in Alfred's day, but in those primitive times the Danes had more often preferred to enrich themselves by direct plunder of place and person. Both sides being now rather more civilized the ransom in gold of the whole country became the usual method of the latter-day Vikings, and the sums extorted from the peasantry were ruinous.

Ethelred 'the Unready' eventually fled the country, taking refuge in Normandy. He had married Emma, the daughter of the Duke, so no doubt hoped he would be treated kindly there. The English asked Sweyn to rule over them, but this Danish leader died soon afterwards, and Ethelred's son, the great Canute, then became King of the whole kingdom. Canute, besides ruling England, was King of both Denmark and Norway. The English soon learned to trust and respect him for he seemed to care as much for their welfare, as for that of his other subjects. The country had peace again for several years.

Canute used this quiet time to make good laws, one of which ordained that all men should assist in the repair of the churches. Thus the restoration of Langport and Huish churches would have become compulsory.

Hardicanute succeeded his father in 1040. His superscription is on coins minted in Langport and now stored in Stockholm Museum. The last name upon Langport coins is that of Edward the Confessor (1042-1066AD), a son of Ethelred, bred in Normandy, who introduced Normans, and who prepared the way for the Norman Conquest.

The town of Langport, being the responsible head of its district, must often have been perplexed in those days of strife, when to follow peace and when war! Its value as a military pass: its position on crown land in a hunting district of the kings, who were constantly renewing the law about keeping up the bridges and fortifications: and Langport's necessity to make constant payments from its mint, would have brought it into almost daily contact with the Court. Then on the 14th October 1066, a small kingdom on the fringes of France, altered the course of history once more, bringing an end to Anglo-Saxon England.

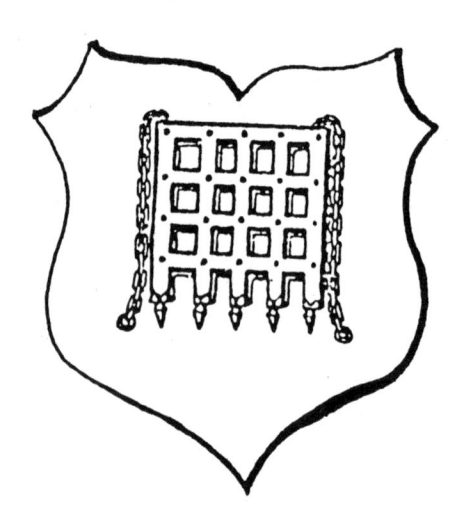

Chapter 6

Norman Conquest - William I - Langport loses its Mint - Domesday Book - River Parrett - Langport's Moors - Henry I (1100-1135AD) Leper Hospital - Parish Church. 1066 - 1154AD

When William, Duke of Normandy, visited his cousin King Edward the Confessor in England, the latter having no son made him some kind of promise that at his death, the crown would be left to him, William. Edward died in 1066. No notice was taken of this supposed promise, and the Witenagemot, or meeting of wise men, chose Harold, Earl of Wessex and son of one of the great earls, to rule over them. Harold spent the whole of his short reign in a struggle to keep his crown, but at Battle, near Hastings, he was killed and his forces overwhelmed by the mailed cavalry and archers of Duke William of Normandy, who conquered England in 1066 and was crowned King at Westminster on Christmas Day.

In many respects the Normans conquered a people more civilized than themselves – Anglo-Saxon England was Europe's oldest kingdom and one of her richest. William the Conqueror inherited a unified country with its own coinage, a standardised language and sophisticated system of government, chancery and law.

Born in 1027 or 1028, William was the bastard son of Robert I, Duke of Normandy, and a tanner's daughter. He became Duke himself at the age of seven or eight, and his early years were harsh indeed. In boyhood his guardians were murdered, and he frequently had to flee from violence. From early manhood his life was spent in the bloodshed of war. William was a large, burly man, unemotional, abstemious and stern to those who opposed his will: a man who engendered little affection but enormous respect. He was also a man of tremendous courage and personal drive, hard-headed and practical, yet uncompromising in gaining his ends. He took an iron grip on the country he conquered, putting down rebellions ruthlessly, resulting in widespread suffering and acute famine.

People of high or low birth, were turned out of their homes and reduced to desperation. Rough Norman soldiers became lords and masters. One could trace the devastation of their march to the West, by the line of ravaged manors left behind them. The West Country did not settle down under the new rule without one final bid for freedom on the hill of Montacute. Men of Langport, some of whom paid dues to the lord of Montacute, would have taken part in the battle, the result being the loss of their Mint. The defeat of the Saxons was followed by hideous penalties – hands lopped off, feet lopped off, and eyes torn from their sockets, all bore witness to the mercy they might expect.

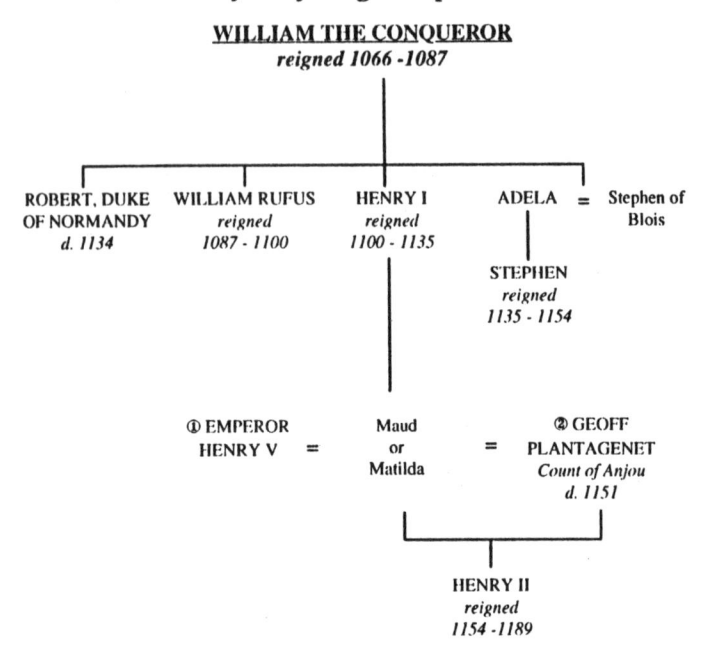

WILLIAM THE CONQUEROR
reigned 1066 -1087

- ROBERT, DUKE OF NORMANDY d. 1134
- WILLIAM RUFUS *reigned 1087 - 1100*
- HENRY I *reigned 1100 - 1135*
- ADELA = Stephen of Blois
  - STEPHEN *reigned 1135 - 1154*

① EMPEROR HENRY V = Maud or Matilda = ② GEOFF PLANTAGENET *Count of Anjou d. 1151*

HENRY II *reigned 1154 -1189*

William revived the *Danegeld* as a tax, and one chronicler says that in 1083/4 he levied six shillings on a hide of land, an exceedingly stiff levy. A hide originally was 'land for one family' but reckoned later in the *Domesday Book* as 120 acres. Five hides were taken as a unit of liability for military service. The Hundred Court, which furnished the profits of fines, and the produce of its area, may have been held at either Somerton or Langport. Six men, with the priest and reeve, attended from each village in the Hundred, and out of these jurors eight were selected, four English and four French, to swear to evidence in the presence of the rest. When a tax was laid on a village by the Hundred Court, the burgesses of the town had to settle among themselves how much each should pay.

The *Anglo-Saxon Chronicle* records that in 1085 '... at Gloucester at midwinter ... the King had deep speech with his counsellors ... and sent men all over England to each shire ... to find out ... what or how much each landholder held ... in land and livestock .. and what it was worth ...'. William was thorough, and *Domesday Book* was compiled in 1086, Langport being listed therein thus '... A town which is called Langport in which 34 burgesses live who pay 15s.: 2 fisheries which pay 10s.: 2 cobs: 9 pigs: 500 sheep.'

William governed directly through sheriffs, the former shire-reeves, removable by the King and acting solely as his officers, and through special Royal Commissioners who for this new rate book went round the counties. Each county, or shire mote, was appealed to on questions of fact. Each Hundred had to answer on oath the questions submitted to it, for example: how much Huish was rated at in hides, who were the tenants, and what were the proceeds due to the King from the borough of Langport. They were required to name the thanes in the time of King Edward the Confessor, and at the date of the enquiry: the number of ploughs employed in cultivating the land: the values under King Edward and in 1066: the amount of forest, meadow and pasture: the mills, fisheries and stone quarries: the livestock: the beech mast or pannage for pigs in the woods: and the nests of hawks. Wild horses, which roamed in earlier years in Langport moor, were still found, according to *Domesday Book*, in Wedmore moors. Serfs and slaves were found among the labourers, who had their own houses and might have held some property with which the lord had not interfered, as long as they had done their duty. Under the Normans, men once free became villeins to a Norman lord, and were forced to cultivate the land. French men everywhere consolidated manors and devised new boundaries. The old system of English society was broken up, and the new came in by which every man was subordinate to a lord.

We also learn from Domesday that Somerton manor, including the borough of Langport, was responsible for providing one night's farm for the King, which meant one day's provisions for his household, *i.e.* definite amounts of bread, beer, cheese, malt, meat, honey and wool, which the reeve had to collect. This 'farm' was commuted for money, so that Somerton with Langport was responsible for £79.10s.7d. The hide was not taxed in addition to the 'farm'.

Langport, a King's town, could not be subject to the numerous exactions of baron or abbot, as was the case with some other towns. The *Firma Burgi*, or farm of the borough of Langport, was a fixed rent paid to the Crown, and all other payments were illegal unless voted by Parliament. Wants were not very extensive and could be supplied mostly in the town – fuel from the woods of Huish (the word means 'wood'), candle wicks from the rushes in the rhynes, and tallow from the sheep. Enough corn for bread and barley for beer was grown. In the pastures of the moors the herds of the township grazed, and 'Langport Field' provided the arable acres tilled in common with yokes of oxen. Cattle supplied leather for harnesses, and the sheep wool for cloth. Milk came from sheep, goats and cows.

River-borne traffic has been a vital factor in Langport's economy from the earliest of days, and from Great Bow bridge the fishermen would set out, and traders to trade, in the Severn Sea, Wales, and southern Ireland. River trade carried down agricultural produce, and brought back metal, mill stones and other rare commodities. William did not change the coinage of the realm, which continued to be the silver penny. Soldier's pay was one penny per day: the value of a fat pig was one shilling, and many plough-lands were let for two pence an acre.

The moors of the Parrett, Ivel, and Tone, with their legions of wild fowl had long been a royal preserve of Saxon kings, who had not interfered with the general right of every subject to slay wild beasts on his own ground. The Normans made the chase the sole sport of a few privileged persons (*e.g.* the King and certain barons), and severe penalties were exacted from any who touched the hare, as well as the buck, for contrary to custom, both animals were made 'beasts of the forest'. Thus, the Forest Court, was brought into existence by the Conqueror – more odious to Norman and Saxon alike than any private jurisdiction, for it represented the King only in his personal and selfish capacity.

In following years, as many as sixty-nine forests belonged to the Crown, totalling almost a third of the whole acreage of the kingdom, about twice as much as Edward the Confessor had owned before the Conquest. The Anglo-Saxon Chronicler wrote: 'He made large forests for deer, and enacted laws therewith, so that whoever killed a hart or a hind should be blinded. As he forbade killing the deer, so also the boars. And he loved the tall stags as if he were their father. He also appointed concerning the hares that they should go free. The rich complained and the poor murmured, but he was so sturdy that he recked nought of them.' Some of the officials of William's court were rewarded with lands close to the Parrett.

The Saxon forest-keepers and other officers were replaced by Normans.

Henry I, William's son (1100-1135AD) who is said to have acknowledged twenty illegitimate children, also made pitiless enactments to protect the birds and beasts of the royal forests, and good ruler as he was, in his reign there was little difference between the penalties inflicted for the slaughter of a man and the slaughter of a stag. The consequence was no sooner was Henry dead, than the first outbreak of the people was marked by raids on the royal forests until no game was left to hunt!

Henry was well acquainted with Langport, Leland (the antiquary) recorded that the King intended to remove the Benedictines from Montacute to Langport, where he would build a very large and splendid monastery. Either the monks didn't like this idea or the King changed his mind. He transferred his generosity to Reading, but he must have taken some steps to start his project. It is probable he stayed in Langport in the course of hunting expeditions. How different the history of Langport might have been if the King's first purpose had been carried out – to build an abbey in Langport!

It has been supposed it was Henry I who founded the Leper Hospital in Langport Westover, opposite what is now the Grange. When in later years Messrs. Bradford built their premises on the north-west of Great Bow bridge, a figure of St. Mary Magdalene cut in Ham Hill stone was unearthed. In the right hand she held a box of spikenard (a herb used in medicine), and in the left a cross. We do know English Leper Hospitals were established after the Conquest. The religious spirit of the Normans was manifest in their care for those who were helpless to face the struggle of life. Lepers had been herded outside the town, in marshes by the river, neglected and cast out. The King probably gave assistance to the building of Westover Leper Hospital because he still retained Langport Borough in his own hand, '... Not thinking it fit to part with so desirable an estate.'

It is possible a church building has stood on Langport Hill since Romano-British days. Few Saxon churches remain not often having been built of durable materials, and the remains of Norman work in Langport church are not sufficient to date the church accurately. If Henry I did build the Leper Hospital, it is possible he built too, the Parish Church in Langport, it being part of the King's manor.

One of the results of the Norman Conquest was the general rebuilding of cathedrals and parish churches, castles, monasteries, halls and manor houses, which arose over the whole length of the country, as if the two

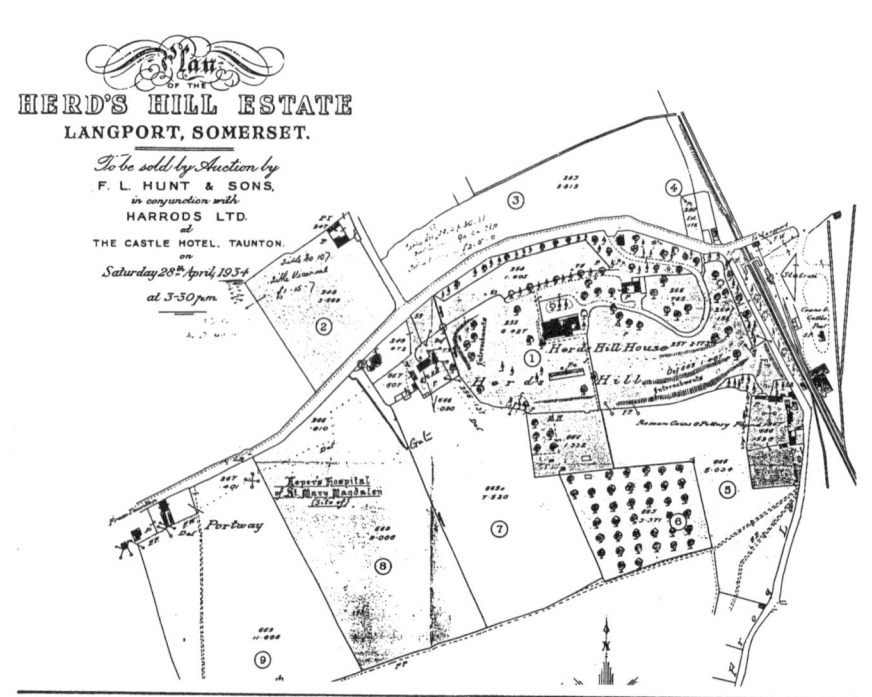

Plan of the HERD'S HILL ESTATE
LANGPORT, SOMERSET.

To be sold by Auction by
F. L. HUNT & SONS,
in conjunction with
HARRODS LTD.
at
THE CASTLE HOTEL, TAUNTON.
on
Saturday 28th April, 1934
at 3-30 p.m.

and a half million population had to a man been apprenticed to the stonemason. The same extraordinary energy which made the Normans the most adventurous conquerors, and the most successful administrators, also made them great builders.

It is said Saxon nobles were given up to luxury. Instead of frequenting the Church in the morning, after the manner of Christians they would spend entire nights and days in drinking. Saxon houses were mean and despicable, whereas Normans lived in noble mansions. The Normans were well attired. They were inured to war, and could hardly live without it, but they revived the observance of religion, and the Norman Conquest, as other invasions before them, had a refining and purifying effect on national life. The Saxon period of six hundred years had been long enough to turn heathenism into Christianity, but had not developed or retained all its virtues.

William's time was divided between Normandy and England, whose language he never learnt, but where he kept such good order a man might travel unmolested through the country with his bosom full of gold, and no man dared slay another, no matter what evil that man might have done him. William died in Normandy from an injury sustained when his horse threw him against the pommel of his saddle. On his death bed, it is said that the man who was 'too relentless to care if all might hate him' wept as he prayed for divine mercy.

Opposite above: Plan of Hurd's Hill Estate, Langport;
Opposite below: Langport Church.

Chapter 7

Henry II - Assize Legislation - Property Sales - Policing - Outlawry - Withy Growing and Auctions - Langport Manor given to Sir Richard Revel - Life in Langport 1154-1199 A.D.

Henry II (1154-1189) when he came to the throne was the most powerful prince in Europe. In 1152 he married Eleanor, Heiress of Aquitaine, recently divorced by Louis VII of France. When her estates of Normandy and Anjou were added to Henry's, the English King ruled a larger share of France than Louis himself. Additionally, Henry reigned over England and South Wales. Before the end of his rule, the kings of Scotland and Irish chiefs owned him as lord. Such great dominions needed a great king to rule and rule well over them, and Henry was just the man. He was clever, firm, and strong-willed, with great bodily strength, and never seemed to fear danger.

Henry's passion for the chase was even greater than that of his predecessors. When not at war, he was perpetually occupied with hunting and hawking. Both Saxon and Norman sportsmen seemed to prefer not the forests of Exmoor or Mendip, but the levels of the Parrett, where the swamps gave abundant hawking and fowling. The best forest, in their eyes, was that which held the crane and heron, the wild duck and other wild fowl.

In 1166, Henry introduced the famous Assize of Clarendon, a new procedure of trial by jury, denying the feudal courts most of their jurisdiction as to the title and possession of land. The Bill protected small landowners whose estates were commonly coveted by some great feudal neighbour. The Norman's favourite 'trial by battle', (always unpopular with the English) meant the parties knocked each other about with archaic weapons of wood and horn, until one cried the fatal word 'craven'. Another custom, trial by ordeal, existed by which the accused had to carry a hot iron for a certain number of paces; if after three days the scar was found to be festering, the accused was guilty. If the scar was clean, he was innocent. Pope Innocent III abolished this last trial in 1215. More often than not, these 'trials' resulted in a wrong verdict and not infrequently an unjust sentence of mutilation or death.

Since the Conquest, the sheriff of each county had tried cases in the County Court. Under the new legislation, Henry began the practice of sending two or more judges from the King's Court, to preside over the County Court. The journeys of these travelling judges were arranged in regular circuits or rounds. In some parts of England, judges still travel on exactly the same circuits.

People were their own policemen. Not only was everyone as curious as they are now about their neighbour's affairs, they were compelled to be so. Every important transaction had to be done in public. A Court was held regularly when all village business was openly discussed. Any man who bought cattle privately ran a great risk of being treated as a thief. The strange guest may not depart in the morning, except in the presence of his neighbours.

In property sales, men did not resort to a lawyer for a deed of conveyance. They registered a sale by instituting a kind of fictitious action in the Shire Court. Thus, when we read of Johannes de Parvo Ponte, (John of the Little Bow Bridge, Langport) buying a house from William Pycot and Cecilia, his wife, the former agreed to give one rose every midsummer to William Pycot, and he paid into court as proof of warranty, one sore sparrow hawk (*sore* meaning one-year-old, worth about twenty shillings). All landed property then involved some feudal or military service to the superior lord. The tenant down to the humblest owner of the smallest piece, owed some service to the lord, who owed service to the king. In receiving the rose – or it might be a clove, gillyflower or peppercorn – William Pycot could prove that John, and not he, owed feudal duty.

Such policing arrangements were aided by the continuing custom of *Frankpledge* set up in the earlier days of Athelstan, whereby each man was made answerable for the life and conduct of others within a group of ten, or the tithing. In theory every man was obliged to be in tithing. Villeins were not. Nor were others who had sufficient security in rank, land or property. The head of the household or community was held responsible for those included in his *mainpast* (household). Every man was required to help in the arrest of malefactors. When someone shouted 'Tom, Tom, the piper's son, has stole a pig and away he's run', then all Bow Street was required to rush out, raise the 'Hue and Cry' and pelt after Tom until they got to the end of the town. Then Curry Rivel would have to take up the running, and so on until Tom was caught. The 'Hue and Cry' was a common way of advertising trouble and securing publicity, but in truth, headed by the portreeve and the constables, it was unprofessional and inefficient. Outside the walls of the borough no-one kept watch. When some offender had been chased to the borders of Devon, for example, Somerset folk would be likely to return home saying 'Let Devon men mind Devon rogues.'

Henry's new justice was popular. The royal writ at least offered occasional help and remedy to the defenceless, yet there was a less attractive side to the new legislation. A large part of the King's revenue was obtained at the Assizes by fines and these, payable on so many counts, were a common grievance, *e.g.* a case concerning Langport itself: 'Walter le Parker was drowned at Langport. No Englishry.' Therefore: murder fine. The jurors presented no 'finder', so they were fined. The 'finder', who didn't appear, was part of a group responsible for him, so the group was fined. Hence the justices made three sets of fines for the royal exchequer from one suit. The expression 'no Englishry' was an enactment of the Conqueror, who was determined that his Norman or French followers should be protected in life and limb. If a man was found slain or dead, it was assumed the body was French until the opposite (Englishry) was proved. Langport did not or could not prove that Walter le Parker was English, therefore it had to pay the heavy murder fine. Possibly he was a Frenchman, and may have had charge of the lord's park! The next Langport case brings before us the old system of Outlawry. 'Roger Harold was suspected of larceny and fled. Therefore let him be outlawed. He was harboured in Langport without tithing. Therefore Langport will be fined'.

Outlawry was very common at this period. The miscreant was driven from the haunts of men. It was every man's duty to capture him. If captured, he could be sent to the gallows on proof alone of his outlawry. His goods were forfeited to the Crown, and his land to the lord, after it had been in the King's hand for a year and a day. For example, when Henry the moor-reeve of Langport was hanged for felony, and after the Crown had enjoyed the profits of his land for a year and a day, it was given to a John de Erleigh. Women and boys could not be outlawed. A child born to the outlaw could not inherit from him, nor could anyone else, for he had a taint in his blood. Anyone who harboured him committed a capital crime. If the King in-lawed him, he came back to the world like a new-born babe, capable of new possessions, but having none of those which he held before outlawry.

Often a man would take sanctuary in a church, rather than become an outlaw, in which case it was the duty of four neighbouring townships to surround the church, and send for the coroner. If the man agreed to confess, the coroner would allow him to travel to some specified seaport, after he had taken an oath at the church gate to quit the realm and never return. He would carry a wooden cross, and travel only on the direct highway, barefoot, bareheaded, and clad only in his coat. He had to embark immediately when he reached the port, alternatively, if no vessel was available, he must wade into the sea to testify his desire to leave, and sleep on the beach, or take sanctuary afresh. So ... when in our neighbourhood, Walter the fairheaded, killed Robert, the basket-maker in 1225AD, he left the land, but returned. The town didn't accept him. It was fined. The Sheriff had to pay over to the King the worth of his goods. Walter was made an outlaw. A man who had taken sanctuary might refuse to confess, or leave the church, in which case a grace of forty days was given him. Two townships had to watch the church day and night. Thereafter, he was dragged forth by lay hands. Taking sanctuary and banishment were both abolished by Henry VIII.

Traditional basket-making.

Perhaps here I should make further mention of the luckless Robert, the basket-maker, murdered by Walter, the fairheaded. What is interesting about him is that basket- making was his trade – his full-time employment – a simple skill in twining willows for some single object, for baskets. fishing pots, and much more, including coracles and even shields. Withies being rigid yet resilient, have been used to brace corsets, to make frames for bearskins (the headgear worn by the Guards), and to provide containers to be dropped by parachute.

Anyone who remembers the old withy auctions in more recent times must regret the loss of them as a social occasion. Traditional custom was for everyone to be given a free pint of cider or beer on entering the saleroom, probably in a village inn. This jolly benevolence extended to individual buyers, who received a token entitling them to another drink after each successful bid. What was auctioned was the right to cut withies 'after the fall of the leaf'. That phrase was part of the conditions of sale: the right being held for one winter only. The following year the buyer would have to bid for the same bed again, if he wanted it a second time. A part only of the price was paid at the auction – anything from a tenth to a quarter. The balance was not due until the end of the season, so giving an opportunity for the man with limited capital to cash his crop before paying for it.

Langport was part of the royal demesne until Henry II in 1190, according to the Hundred Rolls, gave the Manor to Sir Richard Revel (Rivel), Sheriff of Devon and Cornwall, who is said to have obtained a charter for it:

> know that we have given and have granted ... to Richard Revel and his heirs the Manor of Lamport ... to hold of us and our heirs with all their appertances ... Wherefore we will and firmly command that the aforesaid Richard and his heirs after him may have ... the Manor ... for the service of two knights, well and in peace, freely and quietly, entirely, fully and honourably, in woods and in open country, in meadows and pastures, in fishponds and pools, in roadways and pathways, in streams and mills ... with all their liberties and free customs.

Doubtless the King received a considerable payment from Rivel for this charter, as did Richard I (the Lionheart) from Langport, when he ascended the throne in 1189, succeeding his father. Langport received an immediate demand for a 'gift' from Richard, who wanted money to start on the Crusade. He was prepared to sell any and every office to obtain it.

Our forefathers were accustomed to frequent travelling as the Assizes demonstrated, attracting men from every inhabited place in the county. Many roads were so bad as to be almost impassable, although main Roman roads were kept in fair repair, being in constant use. The King himself with his following was often moving about through the land. He rode everywhere, looking after his subjects and seeing that those he placed over them did their duty. The King of France said of King Henry II, 'The King of England neither rides on land nor sails on water, but flies through the air like a bird ...' The stewards of great landlords were perpetually travelling from one estate to another. Humbler folk, traders, and men of business, minstrels, pilgrims, friars, and outlaws, were all to be found on the roads, with vagabonds, thieves and runaways. However well the 'amateur' police worked, the results left much to be desired. Many guilty persons escaped. Life was very insecure and held very cheap.

The general appearance of Langport would have been mean in our eyes. In wooden houses, the floor was of earth, the roof of straw or of reed. Furniture comprised a trestle table, blocks of wood for chairs, or a bench, a rough rack on the wall where fowls could roost at night between the coats and hats, and perhaps a cupboard with wooden platters, cups and spoons. Bedding was sacks of straw. The streets would have been filthy. General cleanliness was unknown. No wonder an epidemic of leprosy marked the thirteenth century, for besides the lack of soap, men had few vegetables, with much salt meat and fish during the winter.

The bridge over the River Parrett at Bridgwater built by Richard I caused problems for Langport's river trade. Gerard said, '... it stopped all shippes from passinge any further to their great benefit but losse of Langport, which nevertheless the inhabitants strived to repair by confining the river within walls and straighter bounds, by means whereof they recovered a greate quantity of very rich land which they enjoy at present ...' Thus river traffic was improved and the new lands (Langport moorlands) helped further industry and the wealth of the town.

Chapter 8

The de Lortys, Langport's Lords of the Manor - Magna Carta - Merchant Guild - Hanging Chapel - Langport's Economic Position - Trade/Wool and Cloth - the de Montacutes - Black Death - Friars. 1199-1349 A.D.

Henry de Lorty succeeded Rivel as Lord of Langport when he married Sabina Rivel. His five sons all married into good families, and traces of his house can still be seen west of the church in Curry Rivel. Langport was valued at £8.7s.7½d. at his death.

Richard I died in 1199, after reigning ten years, only a few months of which were spent in England. His brother, John (1199-1216) ruled so disgracefully that his barons forced him to sign the Magna Carta on June 15th, 1215, which Charter has been the safeguard of English freedom ever since. It was the start of a process which gradually placed the power of the Crown into the hands of the community. John it is said, drank so much new ale and ate so much over-ripe fruit after a disappointing day, that a fever developed and he died after a few days' illness in 1216, regretted by none.

Henry III, king from 1216-1272, succeeded his father, John, when only nine-years-old. His minority was turned to good account, thanks to the honesty and ability of the statesmen exercising power in his name. The first de Lorty's grandson, also Henry, during his minority was a ward of Henry III, who took all into his own hands saying military service was due to the crown. Thus for about twenty years the Crown had a right to the profits of all Henry's inheritance when he became lord of Langport, which included the town.

As soon as Henry III was buried, the barons proclaimed his eldest son, Edward I of England, who had shown by his wise behaviour in his father's lifetime, what type of man he was. His courage and skill in battle was just what the brave English admired.

Edward, a noble upright Englishman, fair and just, was hard-working and anxious to do his best for his country. The young Henry de Lorty seems to have come of age about 1273, and became his devoted follower. With other Somerset men, de Lorty was called to take part in the consolidation of England and under this reign, Wales and Scotland became part of the whole.

In 1321 when Edward II was King, Langport's lord died, and his widow in 1340. Her house, probably the Manor House in Curry Rivel, would hardly have aroused the envy of anyone in Langport now. The windows had only wooden shutters, placed high in the walls to diminish draughts. The floor was earth, rammed down hard and strewn with rushes, possibly boarded at the upper end of the hall. A gutter ran down the length of the room, into which all refuse was poured. Kitchen, granary, stable and hayhouse would have been separate buildings, grouped around the hall and connected by passages. Whale's flesh may have been eaten, or even porpoise, both plentiful in Bridgwater Bay.

Sir William de Montacture of Donyatt inherited the lordship of Langport and Curry on the death of John, de Lorty's son and heir, in the same year as that of his mother. Sir William was created Earl of Salisbury for his distinguished services by Edward III. Langport was fortunate it could claim the protection of so powerful a man. This century saw the beginning of the Hundred Years' War with France. It had long been the custom of the King to hire regiments for his wars from the nobles. The nobles enlisted and maintained soldiers under their private banners, living in their manor houses. De Montacute, probably influenced by the insecurity of the times, fortified and embattled his great house in the second year of Edward III. It was guarded by a moat, and the outer door had a drawbridge attached to it. His fine manorial hall was of a great height, with walls of immense thickness, and he surrounded it with an extensive park.

Edward III laid the foundations of commercial prosperity with his encouragement of trade in wool and cloth. He was obliged to make large concessions to traders to obtain revenue for the wars, and for the pomp of his court. Before his reign, wool had been exported to be made up abroad. Now it was to be manufactured in England. In 1341 the King was granted a tax on the actual wool. Langport was taxed one sack five-stone 10½ pounds – the wool being fourteen-pound to the stone, and twenty-six stones for the sack.

In Langport, John Goldston, dyer, was accused of 'beating, wounding and ill-treating' Alice Damet in Estovere, and of taking from her a stone of blue wool, but Alice herself was convicted of false accusation. More fines! And we have other traces of the cloth trade in Langport. John Bonde, of Lamport, and Gunnild, were indicted before John Thorne, reeve of Yevele, that they feloniously stole six rods of cloth. In 1398 pardon was given to John Swanlond of Bristol, *wolmanger* (wool dealer), of his outlawry for not appearing in the King's Bench to pay his ransom for a trespass done to Thomas Bochere, of Langport. He surrendered to the Marshalsea Prison (in London) and satisfied the said Bochere of his damages. Langport's dependence on the cloth trade was revealed in its rise over the next century from being the eighth to the fourth largest importer of woad through Southampton. Dyeing depended on natural materials, and woad provided the strong colours which remained popular for centuries. The town's inhabitants included dyers, drapers, tailors and cloth merchants.

William de Montacute died in 1344 of bruises received in a tournament. His son, a minor at his father's death, became a ward of the King with the custody of his estates in the King's hands, as was the custom. The young earl went to the French Wars with the Prince of Wales, and was in his division at the Battle of Crecy in 1346 being then, like the Prince, only sixteen-years-old. From his manors in this neighbourhood, the young de Montacute would have found little difficulty in obtaining recruits to follow him. Pardon was granted for their trespasses and outlawries to two Langport men, Roger, son of William le Carter, of Langeport, and Roger, son of William Gilot (Gillett), on account of their good service in the war on France. Yeomen volunteered willingly, being tempted by the high rate of pay, as well as by the hope of rich plunder. The longbow became the prescribed weapon, and the practice at the butts behind the churchyard became the chief sport and excitement of village life. Handball, football, hockey, coursing, cockfighting, and such like, were prohibited by Edward III, as they drew men away from the butts.

Instead of contending on the football field or cricket pitch, young men delighted to follow their lords to war. The sporting nobles of that age entered the battle or lists with high courage and enterprise, and still aching with hard knocks, departed in a most courteous manner from their antagonists, thanking them greatly for their pastime. They were ready and orderly before the battle, restrained in the first moments of victory, and generous in ransoming their prisoners, to whom they would make good cheer and release them on their word to return again with the ransom. But a great gulf existed between the chivalrous baronage, the traders, and the people at large. The strange virtue of chivalry inspired much noble sentiment, but could not conceal general brutal indifference to human suffering. The nobles had neither sympathy nor understanding for the rights and sorrows of the commoners. They harried and robbed and butchered the masses of a hostile nation without any scruple whatsoever.

Between August 1348 and September 1349 came the terrible visitation of the Black Death, which carried off nearly half the population of England. Some villages and hamlets ceased to exist. The plague eventually was stayed, but remained in our island, and was perpetually breaking out in one insanitary township after another – a black cloud, hovering over the filthy streets and brief lives of our ancestors. Half the people of Langport and its district suffered, and the whole organisation of labour was disrupted. The ensuing struggle between capital and labour upset many old manorial customs. A fierce spirit of resistance was aroused among the people, who refused to be tied to the soil or compelled to supply again the old customary duties in the manors of the lords.

Manors of that age had been mainly valuable to the lord, not because they furnished so much money (though they did), but so many men at arms. Villeins were bound to be furnished with arms. Some of them held their land on condition of following the lord to war. The bailiff too would have been a most important person on any manor. Everything depended on his skill and energy. He had to know about every stick and stone on the estate. He recorded the number of nails used in mending carts and ploughs, the shoeing of the mules, the cost of parchment for the Court Rolls, the amount of seed corn, and whether the tenants hoed with their hands or their tools. He also recorded presents given to the King's representative, as well as the money paid for garden seeds and pot herbs.

The manorial system in vogue from the days of Alfred, compelled the inhabitants generally to remain in the parish in which they were born. People lived and died in the same place. Their bones were laid in the sepulchres of their forefathers. The lord of the manor expected his tenants to bring their wives and daughters, as well as their sons, to the work of the manor. Marriages and deaths were entered in the Court Rolls of thousands of manors up and down the land. The custom of manors was perpetuated by the Poor Law of Elizabeth, which required that everyone should be maintained by, and referred back to, his own parish. Those who were unlikely to be capable workers were quickly marched out. Lynx-eyed overseers prevented undesirables from settling. At times the poor

Above: Hanging Chapel (artist's impression).
Opposite: Hanging Chapel, 1994.

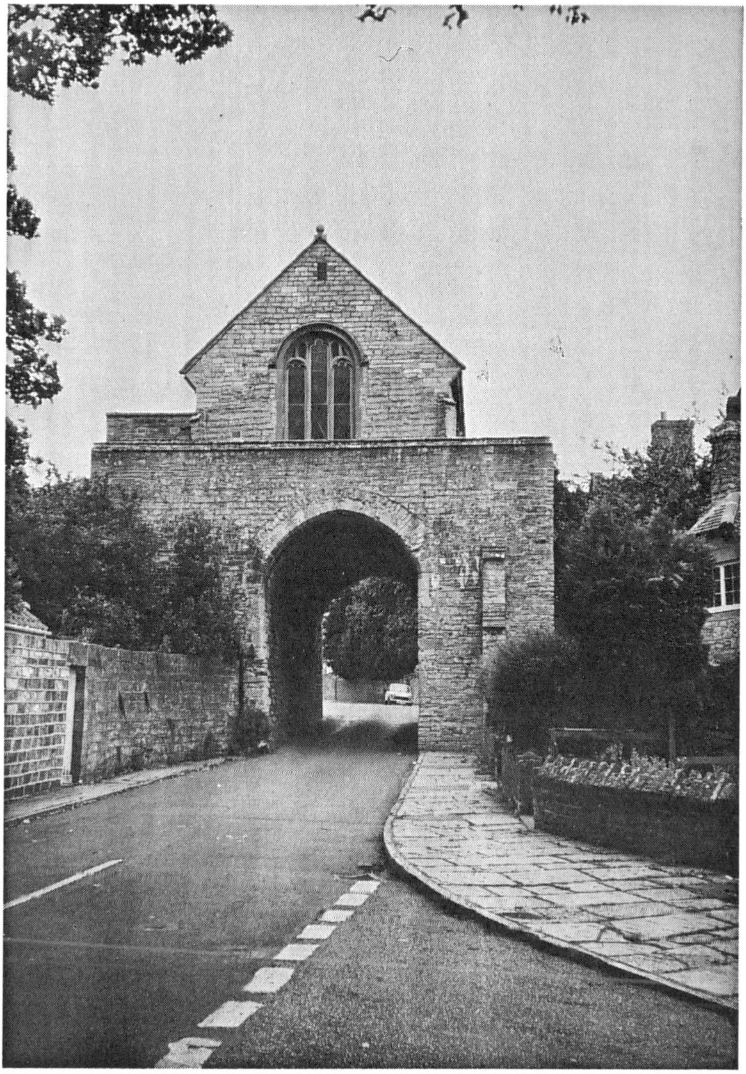

did obtain licences to settle elsewhere, but if these were refused, they were practically imprisoned in one parish. Settlement Acts prevented them from taking their labour to the best market. 'Serfs of the Lord by blood, who with their issue have removed from the lordship without leave' if caught – outlawed and branded with 'F'. Any place which harboured them would be fined £10. If not caught for a year and a day, they would become free automatically under the Statute of Labourers.

Lords themselves could not understand the new system of free competition for labour growing up in place of the old traditions in the working of the manor. Money payments gradually became of great benefit to them and to their tenants. The lord wanted money for his incessant campaigns and the pomp of chivalry, so now he found he need only hire as many men as necessary to work his land. He could allow others to leave the manor on payment of a fine. Thus many villeins became free, and detached from the land. They accumulated holdings and increased the class of sturdy yeomen who became the backbone of the country.

In the same years, another great change was brought about. This time in the religious life of the country by the arrival in England of mendicant or begging friars. Many clergy had given themselves up to lives of ease, and were doing little or absolutely nothing for the poor people in their charge. In our area, Bishop Ralph visited Muchelney Abbey in 1335, and found that the monks had a vineyard nearby from which they made wine. They rode and wandered about the country, and had costly vessels in their refectory and luxurious beds. The Franciscans moved to pity by the plight of the poor, barefoot and wearing the coarsest of garments, went all over the country doing their best to improve the miserable and unhealthy homes in which they lived.

These years were the birth time of the England of today. The House of Commons first appeared as part of the constitution, and the ancient borough of Langport in 1304 was able to send two representatives to Parliament. The town added to its Parish Church, and built its Merchants' Guild Chapel (the Hanging Chapel). The fact that Langport could send representatives to Westminster shows its emancipation from a dependent condition. The town had privileges of its own, self-government, self-taxation and justice in its own borough court. Interference from without was restricted. Merchants formed guilds through which they influenced social and religious life. The Merchant Guild which provided Langport's curious Hanging Chapel (first mentioned in 1344) also provided its fraternity priest, and possibly a second priest in the parish church, at its own expense. The Fraternity or Guild of St. Mary in Langport provided for sickness, old age, poverty, losses by fire, and the education of children, as well as additional spiritual ministrations. It regulated and protected the trade of the town. Langport was a big family of traders, wealthy enough to have their own special Chapel. It arranged for the admission of apprentices. It made laws concerning the quality of goods and their price, tools and methods of work and hours worked.

Medieval shops were built with means of manufacturing on the premises. Living quarters were in the upper storey over the workshop, the goods being displayed on a bench beneath an overhanging porch. The market was always the natural medium of distribution, and records show that increasing numbers of rents were paid when areas of wasteland were granted in 1373-4.

Langport's general economic position in the early fourteenth century in the context of its taxable value stood eighth in the list of county towns, and by 1340 had risen to sixth.

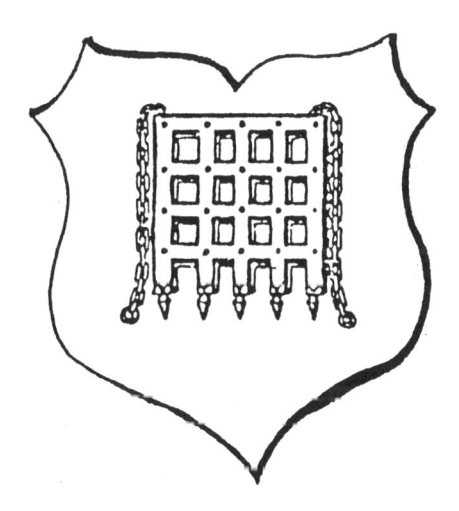

Chapter 9

The Beauforts Langport's Lords - Lollardry in Langport - War of Roses - Lady Margaret Beaufort - Henry VII - Perkin Warbeck Rebellion - Langport Fined. 1349 A.D. - 1509 A.D.

Earl John de Montacute inherited the lordship of Langport from his uncle, in 1397. This noble, high in favour with Richard II (eleven years old when he came to the throne, finally to be imprisoned and murdered in the Tower), was condemned for treachery when Henry IV became the first Lancastrian king. Earl John fled to Cirencester where he was slain in 1400. His estates were confiscated by the new king and awarded to Henry's half-brother, John Beaufort, Earl of Somerset, so Langport came under the direct view of the reigning dynasty. Henry IV issued a mandate to Langport's new lord, '... for the protection of the privileges of the men of Langport Manor ...' who doubtless were trembling in their shoes at the prospect of heavy fines on account of Earl John's rebellion.

In 1410 John Beaufort died. His younger son, also John, then a prisoner in France, inherited the property, becoming Langport's next lord. Ransomed from his French captivity, John in 1443, was created the first Duke of Somerset. His rank and proximity to the throne secured him high command, and once more he was sent to France to share power with the Duke of York. This last expedition proving a failure, Somerset returned home invalided, and committed suicide in 1444. Langport's devotion to its Duke was reflected in the way they engraved his bust on their mace, adorned the staff with his badge of the portcullis and adopted the portcullis as their town seal. In later years, it was set on the battlements of the church tower.

The fierce spirit of resistance aroused among the people after the Black Death, continued. Langport was confirmed in its errors of Lollardry. Lollard was a French word meaning those who sing or mutter, and Lollards were followers of church-protester Wycliffe. He resisted the power of the Pope and papal doctrines. The Lollards' heresy was that later to be Edward IV's trusted minister, so she was allowed by the King to assign certain estates to trustees in her will, including the borough of Langport Eastover and Westover.

After a short illness, Edward died and his younger brother, Richard, seized the crown himself to become Richard III. Richard's cruelty incensed some of the nobles, and is said to have included murdering the two young princes in the Tower, little King Edward V and his brother Richard, by having them smothered with a feather bed. It was not until two hundred years later that the bodies were found, when alterations were made to the building. So Margaret Beaufort's son, Henry Tudor, who was in France, was sent for as being the Lancastrian nearest by right to the throne.

Henry was told if he returned to England and agreed to marry Elizabeth of York, the eldest daughter of Edward IV, he would be helped in taking the throne from Richard. He did return and Richard was killed at the Battle of Bosworth. The crown which fell from Richard's head was placed upon Henry's on the field of battle, and he became the first Tudor king, Henry VII. The houses of York and Lancaster were united. Henry was slight, with a thin face and thoughtful expression, and he had three objectives. He had to rid himself of all rivals to be certain of keeping the throne for himself and his family: he had to weaken the power of the nobles and increase his own strength: and, lastly, he had to ensure he was both feared and respected abroad. Before the end of his reign, he had succeeded in all three.

Thus Lady Margaret Beaufort, Henry VII's mother, became the progenitor of all the monarchs who held the sceptre of England for the next four hundred years, who although she spent her life for her son, never interfered in affairs of state. She rose at 5.00am and spent many hours in prayer. She tended the poor: 'Poor folks to the number of 12 she daily and nightly kept in her house, giving them lodging, meat and drink and clothing, visiting them and comforting them, and ministering unto them with her own hands, and when it pleased God to see them depart, learn to die, and likewise brought them unto the earth ...' Langport may well be content that its church bears the memorial in its portcullis of both the first Duke of Somerset and of his daughter, the best and most saintly lady in England at the close of the medieval period.

Langport owes the restoration of its church, mainly to a supporter loyal to Lady Margaret and a trusted servant of Henry VII, viz a John Heyron (Heron). The perpendicular churches of Somerset were an outcome of the

the Bible alone provided the religion of Christianity. The movement was, to a large extent, independent of Wycliffe, for all over the country there had grown discontent with the ecclesiastics and with civil order. Wycliffe's individualistic views were spread far and wide by itinerant 'poor priests' whose lives and preaching compared so well even with those of the friars, and certainly with the well-endowed prelates.

Earl John de Montacute had put himself openly at the head of the sect. 'He scoffed at sacraments' and had given shelter to the Lollard preachers. No wonder his estates were confiscated by Henry IV, antagonistic to the Lollards, and who passed an infamous Statute for burning them! Many were burned. Lollardism continued. In Langport, people turned out the vicar and refused to have another. It was said Langport people 'neither dread God nor live by the holy church', and they ministered the sacraments and buried the dead themselves. They refused to have a priest, would do no penance, and had beaten up the Bishop of Wells' officers, defying all ecclesiastical authority. Lollardism was forced beneath the surface, but did not die out, and in later years gave impetus to the Reformation.

Under its Lancastrian lords, Langport was brought into close contact with both the French Wars, and the War of the Roses. Lady Margaret Beaufort, both the daughter and heir of the late Duke, was three years old when her father died. She lived to 1509, having had Langport amongst her great possessions for sixty-five years. In 1455 she was married by Henry VI (1422-1461) to one of his half-brothers, Edmund Tudor, Earl of Richmond, who died in 1456, leaving her with an infant son.

Today, if people think the Government is ruling badly, they can vote against them in elections, but in past days men acted differently. The only way they settled such matters was by fighting a personal battle of strength. Richard, Duke of York, became Protector when Henry VI suffered a bout of insanity in the years 1453/54, but when Henry recovered and resumed as head of affairs, the Yorkist lords demanded he dismiss his own lords from the Council. Henry refused and many battles were fought in the struggle for power. In 1461, Henry VI's reign came to an end, and Edward IV, the Duke of York's eldest son, came to the throne.

Edward accused the Lancastrians of treason and confiscated their estates, excepting those of the Dowager Duchess of Somerset and her daughter, Margaret. Margaret's second husband was Henry Stafford, son of the Duke of Buckingham, and her third was Stanley, Earl of Derby, wealth the cloth trade brought to the county, and Langport Church was made one of the most symmetrical and beautiful. John Heron secured a licence to found a Chantry of the Blessed Virgin Mary within it. Both he and his son died before its completion, but it was eventually established in the south chapel of the church. The endowment also comprised lands, including a plot in Langport '... on which the dwelling-house of the cantarist of the said Chantry was built.' Langport churchyard formerly extended further north than its present position, to include the present roadway. Priest Lane led directly into it. Westward of the north aisle of the church stood the market cross, at the bottom of 'Uppstreete'.

Traces of the cloth trade in Langport have already been mentioned. In Henry VII's days it was one of the chief exports. There was hardly a home in Somerset without a spinning-wheel and hardly a manor without half-a-dozen hand looms. Teasels used to brush up the cloth were grown widely in the area. Langport's small foreign community, which it supported in the mid-fifteenth century, mostly from the low countries and France, were often engaged in the manufacture of cloth, which was widespread.

The system of cultivation followed, though, would have aroused the wonder and contempt of a modern farmer. By then, the whole arable land of a village was divided into three great fields, one was sown with wheat, another with oats, and a third lay fallow in one year. After harvest, all the stock was turned out onto the stubble. Most of the animals had to be killed in winter, there being little hay and no roots. Enough were kept alive for essential purposes, fed on the loppings of trees, moss and ivy, but these were much stunted in size. As there were no hedges to protect stock in the spring, many calves and lambs died from the cold. Our sheep of today would outweigh the cattle of those days. Their fleeces only produced one pound of wool.

Another important event which brought excitement to Langport was the Perkin Warbeck rebellion. This pretender declared himself to be Richard, Duke of York, the younger of the two princes imprisoned by Richard III, who managed to escape when his brother was murdered. Warbeck gave Henry VII, unable to disprove this claim, a great deal of trouble. The men of Cornwall rebelled against the heavy taxation imposed to fight against the King of Scotland, who had invaded England. Their numbers were increased by the King's enemies who supported Warbeck, and they marched unmolested through the southern counties, aiming to destroy the King's Council.

A large division of this 'army' passed through Langport, Athelney and Muchelney. Rich and poor, from fear or favour, helped them with food and 'aided and comforted' them on their march. It is said nearly every householder in Langport entertained them with bed and board. The Abbots of Athelney and Muchelney treated them with the same hospitality they gave to all strangers. At Blackheath, within sight of London, the King's forces defeated them, and they were defeated again after a second rising when Warbeck deserted his army and fled.

The King dealt leniently with the rebels, but large fines were imposed on all who had helped them on their way. Langport with the Hundred of Kingsbury, which included Huish, had to pay £426, and the Abbots of Athelney and Muchelney each paid £60. This heavy fine would have been difficult for Langport to bear, after all the other expenses willingly incurred in the restoration of their church. It may have been the beginning of that poverty further increased by the troubles of the Reformation, enabling Edward VI's Chantry Commission of 1547 to describe Langport as '... a market town sore in decaye ...'

During the latter part of the 15th century, the government was strong and capable of keeping order in the country. Great changes had taken place in the reign of Henry VII. For the first time European sailors crossed the Atlantic, and discovered the New World. In 1492 Columbus discovered the West Indian Islands. In 1497 John Cabot, an Italian who sailed from Bristol, reached the mainland of America. In the same year, Vasco da Gama found his way round the Cape of Good Hope to India. The invention of printing made books more plentiful. Peaceful times gave men leisure to read and improve themselves. The England of Henry VII's time began to bear some likeness to the England of today.

Chapter 10

Henry VIII. King's Commission - Reformation - Dissolution of Monasteries - Hanging Chapel becomes Town Hall - Mary - Elizabeth - Langport's Lord of the Manor executed for Treason - Langport reverts to the Crown - Langport granted a Charter by Elizabeth

Henry VII was able to leave his throne without fear of a rival to his son, Henry VIII, then eighteen-years old, when he died. Henry, tall, strong and handsome, excellent at knightly pursuits, could beat his own yeomen of the guard at archery - a very different man from his father. A paragon of princes, he was the patron of all true English sportsmen and of men of learning. It was said Henry's Court had a better store of learned men than any university!

The same bishops, and the same clerics, still performed the same services in the same churches in the years of Reformation. But under Henry, papal authority was abolished in England. Those large revenues the Pope was accustomed to draw from the Church of England were appropriated by the Crown. The Pope could no longer appoint clergy to the English churches, or take appeals from English Courts. The King became supreme Head in all matters, both ecclesiastical and civil. At the same time, in 1535, a Commission was set up to make an accurate return of all church property.

The Commissioners required from every incumbent a full account on oath of his income from every source. Sir Thomas Recitor (Rowseter), Vicar of Huish cum Langport, had three sources of income:

(1) personal tithe, *i.e.* the Easter offering given by each principal parishioner;
(2) tithes from land; and
(3) offerings at celebrations, festivals, marriages, etc., totalling £13. 12s. 8d.

He also received £1 6s. 8d. as tithe on wool and lambs, and his glebe was worth 9s. 4d. (Tithe: one-tenth part increase per annum from profits and industry of parishioners payable for the maintenance of the parish priest, by everyone who had things titheable. Glebe land: the land which belongs to a church as its dowry.) Out of this he paid 7½d. to the young Duke of Richmond, Lord of the manor and Henry's natural son, and 17s. 7½d. fees to the Archdeacon of Wells. In future, a yearly tenth of £1.9s.½d. was to be paid to the Crown, leaving £13. 1s. 4½d. for the vicar himself and the curate, or parish chaplain, whom he had to appoint for Langport. The Vicar of Curry Rivel had £12.8s.3½d. for himself and the curate of Langport Westover Church, which stood in what is now Hurd's Hill grounds. The latter church, probably dedicated to All Saints, was said to be worth £14 by the Chantry Commissioners in 1547.

The Abbot of Muchelney had rents from property in Langport worth £1.15s.4d. per annum, and Athelney Abbey also owned cottages, burgages, gardens and shops in Langport in 1546. Minchin Buckland Priory held land from the fourteenth century near Froggelane in Westover. So when in 1538/9 the order came from Henry VIII to destroy the monasteries, one can imagine the effect this would have had in Langport.

For many hundreds of years the buildings of the monks had been the most noticeable in the country. Even now, though so many have been utterly destroyed, there are numbers of beautiful ruins to be seen, *e.g.* Glastonbury Abbey in our area. But at that time they were all inhabited, and each was the head of a little life in its own neighbourhood. But as times became more peaceful, matters had not always continued to go well. Fewer men cared to become monks, and quiet learned ones, who in former days would have sought the peace of the cloisters, now preferred to go to the universities instead. Many monasteries became filled with a set of men, numbers of whom were quite ignorant and worldly – very different indeed from those who had first built their homes in the wilderness – who had become very rich. Hence the revival of Lollardry, suppressed over a century earlier.

Henry, at war with Scotland in 1542, demanded loans or benevolences from his subjects. Amongst 'the names of the Kinge's subjects within the County of Somerset that haithe granted a lone' appeared two Langport men: Thomas Smith, alias Wever, and John Snow, each paying one hundred shillings. A further six men contributed a sum equivalent to about £240: then other Langport names gave goods, land and money: and so on into 1547. And woe betide any man who spoke about the King's wives. He would soon be squeezed of his money! the King thus ground the tradesmen and others down with taxation. The poor as ever were the sufferers. Many thousands of dependents and farm labourers became deprived of the means of livelihood, and many destitute persons of relief. When the money had all gone, Henry hit upon the idea of debasing the coinage, from which brilliant invention we have been suffering ever since.

There remains some dispute about Henry's true character. Some think he was a heartless selfish tyrant and others that he was a wise and patriotic King. It is certain that in spite of his behaviour, Henry VIII was popular with the great mass of his subjects, even though thirty years of power and worship turned him into a monstrous egoist, moving remorselessly towards a middle policy in religion with royal power substituted for papal power. But there is no doubt with his burly form and strong will, he stands out as one of the most remarkable of our English Kings.

Following the Dissolution of the Monasteries and Henry's death in 1547, the Duke of Somerset (Langport's Lord of the manor) became Protector of the Realm in Edward VI's minority, he being only ten years old. This rapacious Duke led the courtiers who continued the plundering, for there still remained enormous wealth invested in the furniture and accessories of the churches. There were pictures, ornaments, and shrines of gold, silver and precious stones. Even the lead from roofs was taken. Beside this, there was other property in the chantries and guilds, in the hospitals for the aged and poor, and in the almshouses.

This same Duke of Somerset, who had destroyed Glastonbury Abbey and had with some difficulty been prevented from pulling down Westminster Abbey to build himself a palace on its site, introduce an Act, said to meet the expenses of the Scottish War and to build schools and relieve the poor. Some old schools were re-founded and became known as King Edward VI's Grammar Schools, but only a small part of the spoils was used for the general good – the rest went to replenish the impoverished Treasury. 'The Great Pillage of the Church' began.

In Langport, the borough was deprived of its two fraternity priests. The Hanging Chapel was turned into a Town Hall, and the lands and property of Heron's Chantry were seized. In all likelihood the St. Mary Magdalene Hospital of Westover (the original leper hospital), and the borough school, were both then deprived of support. The suppression of the guilds, the benefit clubs of the day, caused widespread distress and increased the impoverishment of the towns, which had begun under Henry VIII. Houses fell into dilapidation. Streets became dangerous for traffic. The condition of the people was wretched in the extreme under Edward VI.

The Protector Somerset had no patience and forced his own beliefs on the people. A very keen Protestant, he demanded church services be said in English instead of Latin, and ordered Cranmer, Archbishop of Canterbury, to translate a new service-book called the First Prayer-Book of Edward VI, which had to be used in all churches. Country people could not bear to see the things they had been taught to revere treated with scorn by the ignorant men sent to make such changes. The book was so much disliked in the West Country that within a week of its first being read, the men of Somerset, Devonshire and Cornwall rose in rebellion. They besieged Exeter for six weeks, but the untrained countrymen were defeated when the King's Council sent troops against them. Exeter stayed loyal to the crown, but numbers of rebels were slain.

The state of the country grew from bad to worse. People longed for the time when the young king would be old enough to rule himself. Edward, very carefully brought up, seemed to have been both good and clever. 'He was so forward in his learning,' it was said, 'he wrote Latin letters to his father before he was eight years old.' Nothing but good was heard of him, and great was the grief of the nation when it became known that Edward was ill and unlikely to recover. He died July 1553. Langport's Lord, the Duke of Somerset, was executed in 1552 for treason, his titles and property attainted, and Langport once more belonged to the Crown. The charge was never proven.

Queen Mary, Henry VIII's daughter, was thirty-six years of age when she began to reign and that was for five years only. When young she was rather handsome, but her life had been a sad and lonely one. Her health was bad, and as she aged she had become sour and discontented. In matters of religion, Catholic Mary was quite sure the old way of thinking was right, and began to put the clock of reform back.

Langport was reminded it would have to report on changes ordered under Edward VI. The portreeve and commonalty were questioned about money paid yearly to their two priests. The Queen desired the restitution of property wrested from churches and parishes, but it was impossible to obtain any clear account of this. The middle and upper classes were determined not to give up their gains. Bad times continued when Mary persuaded Parliament to revive old heresy laws, thereafter, anyone who would not keep to old religious customs was to be publicly burned to death. It is said 300 Protestants were in four years. When Mary died, Elizabeth, the third and last of Henry's progeny, twenty-five-years-old, succeeded to the throne in 1558.

Elizabeth set about partly trying to settle the questions of religion, and partly in doing all she could to strengthen the country. The people had been made so miserable during the last two reigns – firstly by the Protestants persecuting the Catholics, and then vice versa. It was certain anyone who would settle this difficult question in a quiet way would be welcomed. The danger from Rome was constantly in the forefront of men's minds and during the first thirty years of Elizabeth's rule, all England was arming and drilling without cessation. Somerset was taxed by lay subsidies, a form of graduated income tax, as were the monied men and Elizabeth sold or mortgaged many of her properties out of dire necessity. One can understand the feelings of relief and thankfulness when the mighty Armada was destroyed and scattered in 1588.

In 1563, the portreeve and commonalty of Langport obtained a Charter acknowledging their status and confirming to them the tolls of the Saturday market and three fairs, for the express purpose of repairing the bridges within the borough, Queen Elizabeth having 'learned from the piteous petition of our beloved lieges, the Portreeve and Corporation' that the bridges 'are in so great ruin and dilapidation' that the people cannot repair them 'so great is the poverty prevailing among them.' A Court of Piedpoudre to settle injuries was granted in addition. As a market town Langport was connected by its trade and fairs with all the villages around. Customs and tolls might be taken, and all these concessions were to be paid for in hard cash by a ferm of thirty shillings annually to the royal exchequer. It is stipulated in the Charter that no sheriff or other officer of the county molest or disturb the town authorities in the exercise of their privileges. The burgesses themselves could claim freedom from bridge tolls on going in and out of the town, when others had to pay. In return for his trading and judicial rights, the burgess was taxed for town expenses, must serve on juries, muster at arms to defend the town, and serve as portreeve, capital bailiff and constable. His franchise was forfeited if he did not have live in the town or carry out his duties satisfactorily, and he was fined if he did not keep his burgage house in repair. The Charter noted that 'Borough English' was the custom in Langport. Prosperity meant houses could be rebuilt and chimneys added for the first time. An Elizabethan farmer or tradesmen's extravagances (one of them) was in dress. A French traveller in 1558 says, 'Though they have not a crust of dry bread, English women go out dressed in exceeding fine clothes, and give all their attention to their ruffs and stuffs, so that many a one does not hesitate to wear velvet in the streets.' Under Elizabeth's wise government, wealth rapidly increased and a new spirit of enterprise became manifest.

We are not certain who held Langport manor after Somerset's execution in 1552. A John Milner obtained a Crown lease in 1569 of Langport Eastover for sixty years. The next lord of the manor recorded was Hugh Sexey, who obtained a fresh lease in March, 1584. He became auditor to Elizabeth I, and would have been of use in Langport's application for a special Bill to go through Parliament for the purpose of rebuilding the town. The burgesses had sufficient funds at their command, and powerful friends enough, to promote such a Bill. Not content with the condition of the houses and shops, they intended to use their wealth, assisted perhaps by some royal brief or special tax, to re-found Langport on a new and larger scale. The Bill was read a second time, committed in November 1597, and then disappeared. No Bill!

The portreeves exceeded the limited powers granted to them by their Charter. They established two town Courts in the Hanging Chapel, then the Town Hall. They seized felons' goods, claimed the soil of the 'moors', the waste of the manor, the royalties of hunting, hawking and fishing, and elected manorial officers. These claims were contested in the Exchequer by Hugh Sexey in 1600, and the commonalty were eventually threatened with the removal of their Charter if they exceeded their jurisdiction.

The prosperity which marked the close of Elizabeth's reign is seen in the wills. An Elizabethan farmer or tradesman would not have had the many comforts now found in any artisan's cottage. What they had was solid and good, but it would not have taken long to count every article in the house, most of which were mentioned in their wills which often contained bequests to the Church and to the poor. In 1578, Mathew Jefford of Langport Westover, Yeoman, gave

> ... to the relief of the towne of Langport Estover £20 to continewe for ever fore the use and benefit of the poore which will at any time borrow any part thereof bringing sufficient suertye, or pledge to him or them that hath the kepyng of the money for the repaying of it again at the yeares and without usury

or paying of anything for the lone thereof. I give £20 to the relief of Langport Westover ... the money to be derived not from sale of corn, wedge beasts, or rother beasts, but from monies owed to me.

In 1570, I.W. Larcombe of Langport Estover, Yeoman, left to Mr. Vycar of Langport '... a coat or jacket of chamblet with a flatte welte round about the same of velvet ...' and '... to the poor of Langport Westover 20d. to the true maintenance of the poore house 20d. towards the reparacions of the same ...'

Elizabeth died in 1603 after a reign of forty-five years. On her deathbed, she made her ministers understand she wished the crown to go to her cousin, James VI of Scotland. He became the first Stuart King, and James I of England.

Chapter 11

James I - Langport Granted a New Charter in 1616 - Details - the Bridges - Eels - Barge Trade - Langport's Inns - The Harshness of the Age.

James I (1603-1625) was the son of the unfortunate Mary, Queen of Scots, and the great grandson of Margaret, daughter of Henry VII, who had married James IV of Scotland. No-one seemed to have a better right to the throne. Thirty-seven-years-old, he had been a King ever since he could remember, for the Scottish crown had been taken from his mother and given to him when still a baby. Though a Stuart, he was also a Tudor, and the Protestant nobles in charge of James had made sure when he grew up he would be one of the most learned princes in Europe. However, in spite of all his learning, his head became filled with great ideas of the rights and powers of kings. Nor did he behave in a way to win the respect of his subjects. Shabby and slovenly, albeit good-tempered and kind, he was both awkward and ungainly, and ate untidily and greedily.

The Municipal Corporations Commission in their report doubted the incorporation of Langport before 1617. But they had not seen a document in Chancery Proc. Series II in which the Portreeve and Comminaltie of Langport appeared to the Lord Chancellor in 1611 against a certain tenant, William Thomas. Mr. Thomas Snr. had been Portreeve and had held possession of the Charters, letters patents, legers and other evidences of town property on account of suits in which the Corporation was engaged, but had died before delivering them up. Son William kept all these papers and conspired with others '... wholy to disinherit the said towne of the said landes and utterly overthrow the good estate and government of the same towne yf remedye be not had by the help of your good lordship.'

Wm. Thomas rented tenements from the Corporation at twelve shillings per annum under their sealed covenant, but declared that they could never prove their claim against him for want of their charters, etc. The Corporation then asked for a writ of subpoena before the High Court of Chancery. It pleaded that '... the towne is and tume out of mynde hath beene an anncient Burrowe and Corporation incorporate by the name of Portreffe and Comminaltie of the same towne ...' The Portreeve with his brethren had been used to make laws for the Government of the towne, which had been set down in lyger books, and

> ... the said Corporation is seized of and hath belonginge to the same divers messueges, lands, and tenements, within the said Burrow and Towne and elsewhere within the said county of Somerset, the evidences of which landes are enrolled and recorded within the said booke, and whereas also divers and sundry Kings and Queens ... have heretofore out of their gracious and good affection to the said Towne and Corporation ... confirmed to the said Portreeve, Cominaltie, and Towne, and to their successors for ever diverse lyberties and pryveliges for the government, etc. ...

James was the most thorough-going pacifist who ever bore rule in England, and a new Charter was obtained for Langport by grant of the Crown in 1616. It declared that within the memory of man, Langport had always been of that nature and condition commonly called Borough English, and that the Town had divers Charters and Letters Patent from the King's predecessors.

> By whatever name or names they are now incorporate, or have been heretofore incorporate or not, we would vouchsafe by our Letters Patent to make, ordain, constitue, renew, or of new create the same Portreeve and Comminalty of the Borough aforesaid one body corporate and politic by the name of the Portreeve and Comminalty of the Borough of Langport Estover

– they may have a perpetual succession – shall and may have a common seal – may break, change, and make anew their seal aforesaid – and may erect a Counsell house.

The first Portreeve was to be Thomas Lymbere, merchant. There would be two bailiffs, who were to be keepers of the gaol or prison, which should be in the Borough. Power was given to the Portreeve, the Recorder (elected for life), and the ex-Portreeve, to punish scolds, drunken, dishonest, disorderly, and lewd persons. Their authority should be as ample as that of the Steward of the Court Leet.

The Common Counsell or Chief Burgesses should number twelve, and there should be a Town Clerk. The members of the Counsell were to be nominated and appointed as in times past, and were removable for misbehaviour. The Portreeve was constituted Clerk of the Market and Coroner. Toll was granted to the Borough towards the maintenance of the bridges, then in great ruin and decay, *viz* two pence for passing carriages, and 4d. for goods delivered near the bridge or unloaded within six hundred feet of them. Permission was given to seize and distrain carts and boats till the toll was paid, and fines were granted for offences not affecting life or limb.

The Recorder was to hold two courts every year for the settlement of tenements, etc., and for the appointment of officials. Each official had to take the corporal oath on the New Testament. A Court of Record was to be held every Tuesday to take cognisance of debts, trespasses and the like, when fines under £40 could be inflicted. The Sergeant-at-Mace was to attend the Courts and wait on the Portreeve, bearing a gold or silver mace 'garnished and engraven with the sign of our arm.' The freemen of the Borough were discharged from serving on juries or acting as justices outside the Borough.

A fourth Fair was granted and the Court of Pied Poudre was continued. The Sheriff might not enter the Borough or intrude without leave of the Portreeve. The Corporation might hold lands and manors not exceeding the yearly value of £20, and the payment due from the Town henceforth to the Royal Exchequer was to be ten shillings yearly, *less* than in Elizabeth's time.

In James I's reign Great Bow Bridge was spoken of as a 'fair stone bridge of nine arches'. A bequest for repairs was made in 1413, and in 1472 and in 1499 indulgences were granted to those contributing to the bridges restoration when damaged by sea and flood. These contributions included restoring Little Bow Bridge if necessary, which stood where Bow Street now joins Cheapside. The great cost to the borough of repairs was ostensibly the reason for securing a grant of markets and fairs in Elizabeth's time, and the Charter in 1616.

The market was held on the north side of the Hill, immediately west of the former St. Gilda's Convent. A thatched market house was built, then a little house adjoining to accommodate a cage, a pillory, and a poor man to clean the area. By 1596 borough lands included twelve thatched

The Old Custom House.

shambles (shops), a number which decreased to five by 1659.

About 1630 Gerard of Trent wrote that Langport market on a Saturday was full of *peckeles* (eels) as they call them because '... they take them in those waters (Parrett) by pecking an eale speare on them where they lie in their beds ...', eel spears being made by a local blacksmith. Another way of catching eels, now quite definitely out of fashion, was by using cormorants, in a sort of submarine falconry. A noose slipped round the cormorant's neck prevented the bird from swallowing, obliging it to disgorge its catch after each successful sortie. We are told this method of fishing is still employed in Asia. The eel is good staple food, but its offspring, the elver, is a delicacy. When the elvers reach the tidal Parrett in March, they are in size and shape 'like a bodkin'. Enormous numbers run up the river on the big Spring tide, coming close to the banks to avoid the ebb when the tide turns. This gives local people the opportunity to catch them at night with nets made of cheesecloth on withy benders, holding a light behind the net to attract the elvers.

In Elizabethan times, baby eels were stripped, made into little cakes, and fried. Nowadays they are put into hot water to remove the slippery slime, simmered gently for a few minutes, strained, and fried with beaten egg yolks. They can be made into a soup. In the 1960s, the price in Langport for live elvers was only three or four pence a basin, but today there is a large export market and they are wanted to stock eel farms in Europe and Japan, so the price of surplus stock has soared.

Salmon used to be caught in the Parrett by means of trumpet-shaped traps known as 'putchers', made of withies. By progressively narrowing, the traps held the salmon rigid tail-first against the flow of the tide and drowned it. The traps, illegal now except on authorised sites the subject of ancient rights, had to be cleared after each tide if the catch was not to fall prey to the gulls and crows.

Herrings, salt, Welsh coal, grain, and in 1637 iron, on which there was a toll, were brought upstream from Bridgwater by barges. In 1625 the trowermen of that town found themselves barred from their customary beneficial trade with Langport, the plague being so bad. They managed to overcome this and obtain free passage for their goods from Combwich and Bridgwater to Langport, provided no *boteman* entered Bridgwater for food during the pestilence.

ERRATA

p132. 1.13. read 'old' buildings – not 'new'

p124. Walter Quekett's grave – not Rev. Quekett's

p111. 1.22. 'import' of wool forbidden – not 'export'

p123. 3rd. para. omit 'the Rev.'

p127. 1.2. read 'Son William became Rector of Warrington...'

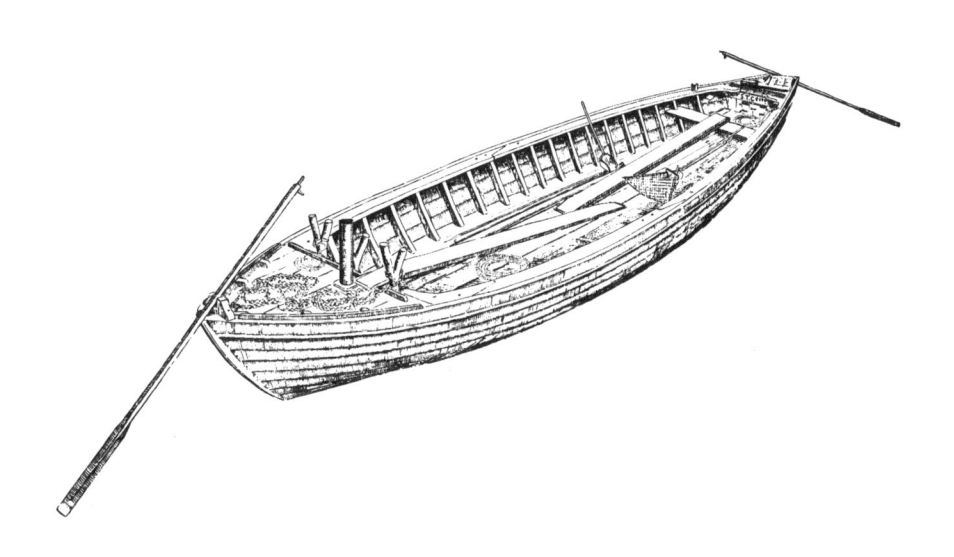

Parrett Barge.

The Quarter Sessions of both James I and Charles I depicted the prevalence of drinking habits and the continuing harshness and inhumanity of the age. For its size, Langport has been well served by inns. The Swan, now the Langport Arms, was an inn in 1596, and an Excise Office was there in 1715. John Michell leased the pub from the Borough which was held by his family until about 1800. The George on the south side of Bow Street, was later converted to a dwelling-house, as was the Red Lion, east of Whatley. The Nag's Head, in about 1692, stood on the north side of the Hill near its junction with North Street. It changed its name to the White Horse and eventually became a private house. The present Custom House in Bow Street was formerly the Angel Inn, but there was another Angel Inn in North Street in 1725, as well as the Five Bells and the Black Swan and the Carpenter's Arms, the Dolphin in 1778 and the Lamb in 1779. The White Lion still standing on the west side of North Street probably dates from about 1786, and the Admiral Vernon near the west door of the church was bought by Vincent Stuckey in 1817, later to become St. Gilda's Convent. As well as the Castle inn now called Hill View, there were five beer houses in Bow Street! Langport was well served, and there were others.

The times were harsh indeed. It is recorded that in 1608, John Bayley of Muchelney, petitioned against the two bailiffs of Langport, William Crocume and Humphry Spurll, who seized his horse and lading for a debt due to Henry Democke, of Langport, and '... they did beat him and break his head that the bloud ded kume downe about his yeares', and yet not satisfied, they did throw him down and did beat him again most cruelly. In 1613 it was ordered that Sir Edward Hext of Low Ham take surety of Cuthbert Searle of Langport (a slippery person!) never to tipple again, and that his alehouse be suppressed.

G. Stuckey of Muchelney, mother of the child Dorothy, was to be whipped at Langport on a Saturday up and down the market 'until her back be bloody.' This was not an unusual sight in Somerset towns. And such women could be sent to the nearest House of Correction to the ruin of body and soul. Apprentices were beaten, starved and ill-treated. Gaols were very hells on earth. 'The contagious and loathsome air' was mentioned in connection with Ilchester prison. The water from the river flooded the rooms, and debtors were thrust amongst the worst criminals.

Langport had its prison, Little Ease, erected in the late sixteenth century. In what is now a space for market stalls under the Town Hall, can be seen still a small black door which lead at one time to the gaol.

It was probably about 1589 when the Leper Hospital at Langport Westover became an 'Almeshouse'. About the year 1622, for some reason, it became obnoxious to the Magistrates, who made an order that R. Warren, the person in charge, should leave and settle at Lyng. When the latter disregarded the order, the Sheriff, a Mr. Marmaduke Jennings, was asked to have the man put out with his wife and children, and sent to Lyng. A whole year went by and Warren was still in the Almshouse. The Judge of Assize therefore confirmed the order, and asked Lyng to find the man both house and work.

One January a complaint was made by the poor people of the 'hospital of Langport' that William Fisher, their governor, and received £60 in two-and-a-half years, but had only in this time spent £20 on them. The rest had been spent in riotous and lewd living, and William Fisher had treated them, men, women and children, most cruelly. Nothing had been done by the following July, when Sir Robert Phelips, Arthur Pyne and T. Lyte were all asked to look into the matter. In those days, disputes could be carried on from reign to reign.

Chapter 12

*Charles I - Revival of Law of Knighthood - Ship Money -
Civil War (Royalists and Parliamentarians) -
Battle of Langport, July 10th 1645 - Cromwell*

Twenty-five-years-old when he became King, Charles I (1625-1649), handsome and dignified, both looked and spoke like a king. Delicate as a child, his lessons had often to be excused and constantly indulged, he had grown up not only very wilful and obstinate, but he was deceitful. He made promises without the least intention of keeping them, and struggled to get his own way without paying heed to the wishes of his subjects or the law of the land.

When Charles married the King of France's sister, Henrietta Maria, he felt strong enough to renew the war with Spain. To obtain necessary funds, he called Parliament and asked them to vote him a large enough supply. But the government would not give the King all he asked for without knowing exactly how the money was to be spent, and who was to have the spending of it! Instead of granting Charles certain large taxes for life as had been the custom with previous new kings, the Commons had only granted him taxes for one year and, instead of making laws against Roman Catholics less severe as the King wished, the Commons insisted they be made even harsher than before. Charles, angry at this reaction, dismissed Parliament, managing with the help of his courtiers to collect enough money by unlawful means to fight the Spanish.

The first expedition sent against the Spaniards was a terrible failure: the ships were bad: the food was bad, and the soldiers were unwilling to fight. It being hopeless to continue without more funds, Charles was forced to recall Parliament, who were both angry at his unlawful behaviour and that English soldiers had failed to win any successes. Parliament refused to give the King money unless he made certain promises. Once more they were dismissed.

Langport experienced Charles I's mis-government in his extraordinary

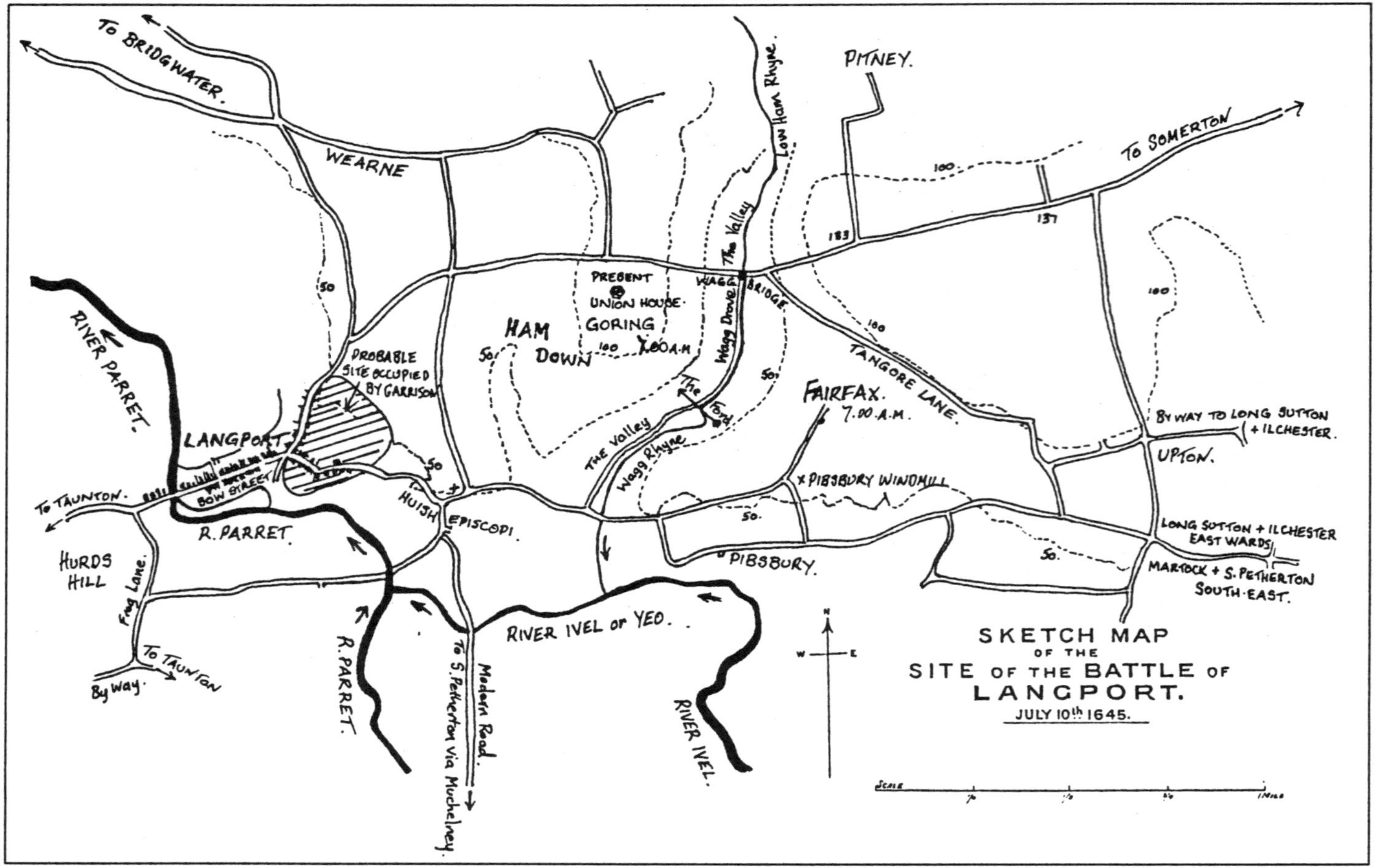

SKETCH MAP OF THE SITE OF THE BATTLE OF LANGPORT.

JULY 10th 1645.

methods of raising cash, one being his revival of the old law of knighthood. Many gentlemen of means were forced to receive the 'honour' of knighthood – and had to pay for the privilege. Many being unfit for that rank, preferred to pay a fine. For example, John Tucker, gentleman, lay rector of Huish, paid a fine of £23 to the collector. Fines and rents were demanded from those who were said to have encroached on the Royal forests and Crown lands. Langport anciently demesne land of the Crown had to pay thirty shillings and was involved in the dispute about ship money.

Previously in times of war, seaport towns paid a tax, ship money, to provide ships and/or money for the King's service. Now Charles ordered this tax should be paid to him yearly by inland as well as seaport towns – whether there was a war or not. The Sheriff assessed Langport, Muchelney and Midney at £20 jointly, out of the £8,000 demanded from Somerset, but although Langport paid £7 12s.4d., the constables of Muchelney and Midney refused to pay the rest, and the Sheriff had no power to compel them.

Member of Sealed Knot.

Before long the King was in fresh trouble. Ever since the French found out he had not been able to keep his promise of alleviating the laws against Roman Catholics, they had been growing less friendly, and eventually war broke out between the two nations, managed as badly as that against Spain. For the third time Charles had to call a Parliament and ask for help. This time the members had decided a stop must be put to the King's wrong-doings, and made him sign the famous 'Petition of Right', in which he had to agree not to tax his subjects, or make them give or lend him money without their consent.

Finally Charles made up his mind to rule alone, and did so for eleven years, but, by now, the country was slowly drifting into Civil War, in which mainly religion decided on which side a man fought. Those who wished worship of the Church of England to remain unchanged, including Roman Catholics, took the part of the King; those who supported the Puritans and wished to have it altered (which meant doing away with the bishops altogether) took the side of Parliament, *i.e.* Royalists and Roundheads.

One wonders whether Langport was Royalist or not! When Parliament had the upper hand, the Corporation sent presents of fish and sugar loaves to their leaders in the area. When the King had the advantage, Langport willingly contributed and sent presents to the Royalist leaders. Probably its main concern was to arrange its affairs so it might hold its goods in peace, but it was held securely as a Royalist town from June 6, 1643, to July 10, 1645, the Battle of Langport, the turning point of the war in the West, when Somerset was lost to the King.

Early in the summer of 1643, Sir F. Mackworth had been made Governor by Sir Ralph Hopton, who had overall command in the Western counties. Langport with the villages around it came under his martial law, being important for the storage of arms and provisions, as a Royalist place of refuge, and a defence along the line of the Parrett with Bridgwater. Fortifications were raised around Langport Hill.

In 1645, Prince Rupert, Charles I's nephew, sent the dissolute Lord Goring as Commander-in-Chief, replacing the chivalrous Hopton. It would appear Goring purposely oppressed Langport to gratify his spite against both Sir Ralph whose success in battle was unblemished and against Mackworth, with whom he had disputed in earlier days. Goring took away all the contributions assigned for Langport's support using them for his own army, and forbad Mackworth to levy the rates allocated to it. At one time the garrison was brought so low it had only two days' provisions!

The Royalists were in a strong position in Somerset early in 1645 – and controlled all towns except Taunton. Clarendon believed that if the King himself had come West after his defeat at the Battle of Naseby, the struggle might have been prolonged, but Goring and his intolerable crew were left in command and ruined the royal cause. Five to six thousand clubmen, people of Somerset and Dorset, formed into an organisation to protect their counties from the depredations of either army, complained to the Prince of Wales of the extreme oppression and rapine carried out by Goring's cavalry. The Prince promised reforms, but forbad such gatherings of clubmen unless they formed themselves into royalist regiments. The importance of Langport is given in Clarendon's words: 'Lamport if it had not been with great industry discountenanced and oppressed, as is said before, might well have secured Goring's and resisted Fairfax's army.'

The Parliamentarian army with Sir Thomas Fairfax and Oliver Cromwell at its head had no hesitation about crushing the King, and so we come to the Battle of Langport, with the forces of Goring opposed to the troops of Fairfax. At sunrise Fairfax was astir, and drew up his army in battle order near Pibsbury Mill: Goring was posted upon Ham Down. Between the two lay the valley through which ran Wagg Drove, then a muddy trackway.

Cromwell's own letter to Sir Harry Vane headed 'Langport. July 10, 1645' related the events.

> *Dear Sir, I have now a double advantage upon you, through the goodness of God ... we have seen great things in this last mercy - it is not inferior to any we have had; ... we were advanced to Long Sutton, near a very strong place of the enemies called Langport; far from our own garrisons, without much ammunition, in a place extremely wanting in provisions ... Goring stood upon the advantage of strong passes, staying until the rest of his recruits came up to his army with a resolution not to engage until Grenville and Prince Charles his men were come up to him. We could not well have necessitated him to an engagement nor have stayed one day longer, without retreating to our ammunition and to conveniency of victual. In the morning word was brought us that the enemy drew out – (We did so.) with a resolution to send most of his cannon and baggage to Bridgwater; which he effected; but with a resolution not to fight, but trusting to his ground, thinking he could march away at pleasure. The path was straight between him and us; he brought two cannons to secure his, and laid his*

musketeers strongly in the hedges. We beat off his cannon, fell down upon his musketeers, beat them off from their strength, and where our horse could scarcely pass two abreast, I commanded Major Bethel to charge them with two troops of about one hundred and twenty horse, which he performed with the greatest gallantry imaginable; beat back two bodies of enemies' horse, being Goring's own brigade; break them at swords' point. The enemy charged him with near 400 fresh horse. He set them all going, until oppressed with multitudes, he break through them, with the loss of not above 3 or 4 men ... Bethel (and Major Desborough) faced about and they both routed at swords' a great body of the enemies' horse, which gave such an unexpected terror to the enemies' army, that set them all a running, our foot meantime coming on bravely and beating the enemy from their strength. We presently had the chase to Langport and Bridgwater; we took and killed about 2,000, broke all his foot. We have taken many horses and considerable prisoners. What are slain we know not ... we had but seven regiments with us. Thus you see what the Lord hath wrought for us. Can any creature ascribe anything to itself? Now can we give the glory to God and desire all may do so, for it is all due unto Him. Thus you have Long Sutton mercy added to Naseby mercy ... God was pleased to use his servants; and if men will be malicious, and swell with envy, we know who hath said: 'If they will not see, yet they shall see, and be ashamed for their envy at his people'. ...

I am going to the rendezvous of all our horse, three miles from Bridgwater; we march that way ... We have taken two guns, three carriages of ammunition in the chase, the enemy quitted Langport - when they ran out of one end of the town we entered the other. They fired that at which we should chase, which hindered our pursuit, but we overtook many of them. I believe we got near 1,500 horse. Sir, I beg your prayers. Believe and you shall be established.

I rest your servant, Oliver Cromwell.

The flight began abut 1.00pm. Goring fled with a thousand horse through the fortifications of Langport, but had not had time to destroy the bridges. His men fired the houses in Bow Street by the bridges '... but our men were resolved to pass through fire and water after them ... the Lt. General himself (Cromwell) following them though the fire was flaming very hot on both sides of him ... there being 20 houses in all burnt down..' Fairfax pursued the enemy through Wick and Stathe, '... and marched through their owne flame with them back again into Langport shewing them their wickedness.' (Fairfax's letter to Parliament refers).

The day of battle over, the houses in Bow Street lay in ashes. The Market Houses, Town Hall, Market Cross, Hanging Chapel and the bridges all required restoration. The dead needed burial: the wounded were crying for help, and the highways were filled with carcasses. At Great Bow a great slaughter had occurred, with the largest capture of prisoners. Fairfax and Cromwell moved on to besiege and take Bridgwater. The story goes whilst they were both surveying the town in a boat, the Parrett Bore all but capsized them. After the Battle of Langport, the Royalists were '... both in the West and in other places destroyed by pieces without either conduct or honour ...'

In Langport, the Portreeve repaired the injured buildings 'tylinge' the market Cross, railing the bridge at Broad Bow, and spending heavy sums at law. The fortifications in North Street were dismantled, and new trestles were bought at great expense for the market.

Now the King was beaten, Parliament and the army fell out. They too could not agree about religion. Whilst Puritan members wanted everyone to follow their severe rules and worship alike, the soldiers thought men should be free to worship as they thought right. The army openly rebelled, took Oliver Cromwell as their leader, and refused to have anything more to do with Parliament. But both the army and Parliament wanted the King's support. He made promises to both whilst secretly trying to rally Royalists in England and Scotland. Before long the second Civil War broke out, lasting from April to August 1648. For a time Parliament and the army had to forget their disagreements and jointly put down this second rising.

So – Charles I was finally beheaded in 1649, and for eleven years the country became a Commonwealth.

Oliver Cromwell.

Chapter 13

Cromwell, Lord Protector - Court of Survey of Langport Corporation's Tenants and Possessions - Restoration - Berkeleys Langport's Lords of the Manor - John Bush - Langport's Town School - Gillet Endowment - School Life

After Charles' execution, both Cromwell's army and the people wanted order restored as soon as possible. The Council appointed to carry on the work of government, did not act quickly enough to please anybody. Finally, Oliver Cromwell with a company of soldiers, whom he left at the door, marched down to the House of Commons, walked in, dressed in his usual 'plain grey suit and grey worsted stockings', and sat listening quietly. Then rising to his feet and speaking with gathering wrath, he accused the members of injustice, selfishness and neglect of duty. He called to his men who rushed in, and turned the members out of the House. Locking the door, Cromwell walked off with the key in his pocket. The ballad-makers chanted:

> *Brave Oliver came to the House like a sprite,*
> *His fiery face struck the Speaker dumb:*
> *'Begone', said he, 'you have sate long enough,*
> *Do you think to sit here till Doomsday come?*

In 1653 Oliver Cromwell became the rule of England with the title of Lord Protector.

Parliament proceeded to dispose of the persons and property of their countrymen. Many estates of Royalists were confiscated. Many honourable families disappeared, and many new men rose rapidly to wealth. Captured Royalist soldiers were shipped to the West Indian plantations to labour in the heat of the tropics, were made galley slaves, or were sent to enforced military service under the Roman Catholic Republic of Venice.

In 1650 there was a Parliamentary survey of Church estates in Langport and Huish, under an Act for the Abolishing of Deans and Chapters, Canons, etc. in the hands of the Ecclesiastical Commissioners. Large domains belonging to the Crown, to the Bishops, and Chapters, were seized, either granted away, or put up for auction. Prices were often nominal, money being scarce and the market glutted.

Warehouses had been built in Langport around the main landing place on the Parrett by Great Bow, with a storehouse and thatched Salt House (Rock House). Quays probably lay along Bow Street's southern side at some time, served by the back river which had been cut.

In 1658/9 a record was made of all Langport Corporation's tenants and possessions including weights and measures. Ten houses were listed between Little Bow and Market Cross, as burgages. The Corporation appeared to have had six houses in North Street, one only being a shop. The rest of the burgage tenements were grouped under Up-Street, otherwise Cheap Street. Watley Close, Frog Lane and Cocklemoor. A withy bed and pasture in North Street came under the manor intrinsecus of the Corporation. The house on the Hill (called 'Mill House') was one of the three houses in the tenancy of the Town Clerk, Thomas Trevilian.

Orders came from Parliament to prohibit all use of the Prayer Book (reading it was judged as great a crime as perjury, drunkenness or fornication). The Quaker movement had come into being, and free congregations of a more fanciful kind had multiplied. The use of the burial service had also been forbidden. In Langport churchyard, the body was committed in silence to the grave. Nor could marriages be solemnized in the Church. The banns were published in the Market Place. The parties then came before a Justice of the Peace, took one another by the hand and made a short declaration.

The Rev. Cananuel Bernard was turned out of Huish-cum-Langport, but continued to celebrate church services, in spite of all possible penalties, in Pitney. The whole countryside seems to have been married by him – not only 45 weddings in Langport, but 24 in Huish, 43 in High Ham, 92 in Somerton – in all 85 parishes. He used the baptismal service too, and dared to enter in 1649: 'Richard Bernard, the son of Cananuel Bernard and Dorothy, his wife, being the 20th child.'

Overall Cromwell's rule was wise, firm and successful. He made his power felt not only at home, where he tried to bring order out of chaos, but abroad, where he was both feared and respected. When he died on September 3rd 1658, many thought the best way to restore harmony was to bring back the Stuarts as soon as possible.

Charles II, then Prince Charles, and his Royalists were soundly beaten at the Battle of Worcester in 1651. Charles escaped and, it is said, disguised as a peasant, spent a day hiding in an oak tree. Though few Royalists had dared to take up arms on Charles' behalf, they had been willing to run great risks to save his life. A thousand pounds reward had been offered to anyone who gave him up. Though many knew where he was, no-one could be persuaded to betray him. Six weeks after the Battle he sailed in a small boat from Brighton to France. Years later he was called back from exile. This time it was not the King who summoned Parliament but Parliament who summoned the King. So eager was it for the King's return, they did not even wait to make him promise to rule wisely, and Charles II entered London in triumph on his thirtieth birthday, May 29th, 1660.

At the Restoration Sir Charles Berkeley was owner of Langport manor. His second son Charles, who had faithfully served Charles II in his troubles, became Baron Botetort of Langport, but when slain in 1665 and with only one daughter as his heir, the baroncy died with him. His father became Viscount Fitzhardinge.

The Corporation of Langport was full of loyalty at this time. The Portreeve seems to have attended the Coronation officially. The entry in the Minute Book read, in 1660, '... cloth and cord to pack up ye mace to send to London 9d. ...' Other rejoicings were recorded at the Restoration. 'Hogshead of beer when the King was proclaimed £1.10s. Beer when the Coronation was observed 5s. For the Company of Masters (burgesses) at feasts and meetings, for wine, beer, tobacco and cider £7.10s.6d. ....' John Blake succeeded as Portreeve late in Coronation year, and the town was still keeping up its rejoicings. '... Hogshead of beer £1 10s. For wine and beare before and after the Masters and Captain went to Church 8s.6d. Dining with the Captain 5s. Quart of wine for the Captain 2s. ...' The arrears of the Portreeve's accounts were brought up-to-date and £2. 14s. was spent in diet, beer and wine to help work along. The income of the town was £75. 6s.

The Corporation again purchased arms, bills and pikes, swords and muskets. John Michell, Portreeve and Landlord of the Swan (now the Langport Arms) indulged in a little finery for the Sargent's Cloake, £1.18s. The town was recovering for it could pay £16 for keeping two Courts of the Portreeve, and for wine. Other expenses included '... To Captain

Cannon for three muskets £1.13s.6d. ... Mowing the river and throwing the hasick 10s. ...' (*i.e.* sedge and rushes to make hassocks). '£2 was paid for the King's arms, which were probably set up in the Church. Three days' pay was given to the trained soldiers, and musters continued.

John Bush, a Puritan and learned man, was minister at All Saints Church for four years, and a great character in the town. He was dispossessed by the Act of Uniformity in August 1662, when he and others refused to obey the laws and constitution of the Church which had ordained him to the ministry. Bush endeavoured to make provision for a growing family by keeping a grammar school, but there is no positive evidence that this was Langport Grammar school. He would have had some respect in Langport as being one of its tradesmen. John Bush's wife, formerly Mary Alsop whom he married in 1662,

> ... being a mercer's daughter of that town (Langport), applied herself to the business she had been used to under her father, and by a blessing on their diligence and frugality he was enabled to make a plentiful distribution to their children, which he cheerfully did as soon as they were capable of employ, reserving to himself only a little to keep him handsomely where he lived ...

The mercer was Humphry Alsop, Portreeve in 1652 and 1656/7, whose family tomb is in the Church near the pulpit. Amongst the Taunton Museum trade tokens is one by John Bush. Farthing tokens were used in the district for necessary change when the shop's credit was good, since the State did not coin sufficient coppers. Before palsy disabled him, John Bush was said to have had great powers of conversation. In February 1676 he was a burgess, later fined ten shillings for refusing to take the oath of allegiance to the King (Charles II) or to swear he would not bear arms against him. In March he was fined £4, in April £5, and in May £10. In July 1678 on pain of a fine of £20, he seemed to have submitted. He took both the oath and the office of magistrate and became licensed to preach in 1672. He died in 1712.

The Puritan Movement was in earnest about education. Under its influence the founding of schools went on much more rapidly in the first half of the seventeenth century than in the previous hundred years. The Langport Corporation Minute Book speaks of the Town School in 1668 as an 'Ancient Schole' and states that the Corporation had recently restored the buildings and that they, the founders of Langport Grammar School, had appointed a schoolmaster. The School received a boost in 1675 with the bequest of an endowment from Thomas Gillet. This provided a salary for the schoolmaster, enabling the scholars to be educated free of cost to their parents. Thomas Gillet was butler to R. Hunt, who was made executor of this generous bequest, and £413 was applied to the Charity.

Hunt not only put in and maintained a schoolmaster, but made laws for the government of the school. There was some dispute with the Corporation who instituted a lawsuit in 1686 complaining nothing had been done for the school for three years. The schoolmaster they appointed had been abused and turned away by Hunt's representatives. Eventually the Court ordered that the ordinances drawn up by Hunt should be complied with. These are of interest as they show the inner life of schools in the reign of Charles II, as well as the piety of both R. Hunt and of his servant, Thomas Gillet.

> The Schoolmaster to be a pious, able, sober and discreet person, above the age of 23, not curat or viccar, nor with charge of souls besides scholars, which charge will be enough for him.
>
> If the Schoolmaster be convicted of the odious sins of drunkenness, profane cursing or swearing, he shall forthwith be removed.
>
> He shall take no pay for the youths of Langport but for such as come from other parishes. In particular the youths of Langport to be taught to read well, write and cast account well, and be well instructed in the Church Catechism and principles of religion, which the master is to do every Saturday after dinner and every Sunday and Holy Day morning before church.
>
> The scholars are to attend 6.00am summer and 7.00am winter, and first thing in the morning and last thing in the evening shall be on their knees in prayer - the Commandments on Wednesday and Friday - the Creed on Tuesday, Thursday and Saturday - and every morning the Lord's Prayer and '... for the King and all in authority under him ...'

The scholars to be at the school 9.00am Sundays and thence with the master to church to be there at confession, and to continue there devoutly and humbly and reverently during the whole time of divine service and sermon, and take notes of the sermon; the like also in the afternoon: and the master to call scholars to an account of the Evening Prayer what they had observed of the sermons. The Psalms for the day to be read every morning and afternoon by the master and scholars alternatively, and before they depart in the evening the scholars to read a chapter by turns, each scholar looking upon his book the whole time, the master very carefully to observe that each pronounces his words distinctly and marks the stops, and that his scholars perform all their services to Almighty God with all due reverence, humility and devotion both in the school and in church.

The scholars to demean themselves mannerly and modestly, not to come uncombed unwashed or slovenly, and to be severely punished for evil acts and words. Each scholar at entrance to do reverence to his master before he sits down in his place, and the master always to demand reverence for his person, though himself kind and moderate in his corrections.

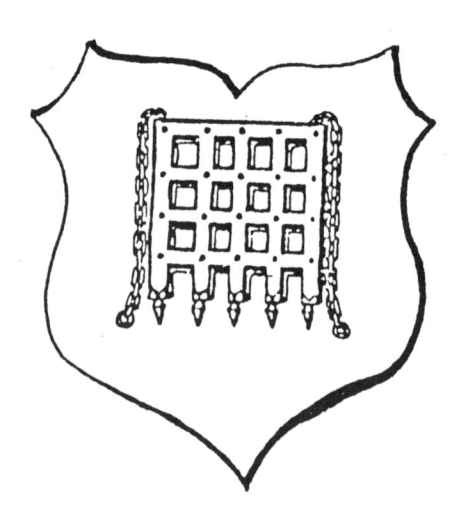

Chapter 14

James II. Monmouth Rebellion - Judge Jeffreys - Bloody Assize - Langport Men Hung and Quartered - William and Mary - Langport Signed Oath Roll - Langport Manor Update.

Charles II died a Catholic on February 6th 1685, and his Catholic brother James II was allowed to succeed him, in spite of fears many felt on account of his religion.

Before he became King, James had shown himself to be a brave soldier, a clever naval officer, and a good man of business, but he did have some very bad qualities. His temper was hard and unforgiving. He was obstinate, self-willed and, like his father, proved unable to understand his subjects' feelings. He seemed to think because he was a King, he could do as he liked. He began to turn Protestants out of their posts and give them to Roman Catholics. People soon learned to distrust him, and then to hate him. He managed to alienate 'not only those classes who had fought against his father, but those who fought for him.'

Many did not mean to give up their hopes of a Protestant King without a struggle. A rebellion was planned to put on the throne the Duke of Monmouth, the eldest but Protestant son of Charles II who had been born in Rotterdam but who, being illegitimate, had no real right to the crown.

In June 1685, the Duke with a small army of followers landed at Lyme Regis from Holland. He said he had come to secure the Protestant religion and to get rid of Popery. Pleased with his promises and won over by his agreeable person and manners, numbers of peasants, including recruits from Langport, flocked to join him. The Duke marched through Somerset and was royally received in Taunton, which was mostly Protestant. The townspeople went wild with joy, it is said, strewing his path with flowers, and maidens of the best Taunton families presented him with flags they had made with their own hands. They gave Monmouth a Bible, which he kissed, saying he had come to defend the truths taught in it and to die for them if necessary.

From Taunton where he was proclaimed King, Monmouth marched towards Bristol, everywhere being received with joy by country people, although few of the nobility joined him. His army grew to nearly four thousand in number. By this time, however, the King's forces were in close pursuit. Lord Churchill based his forces at Langport in June when harassing the rebels on their march northwards. Monmouth, not wanting to risk a pitched battle with well-trained troops, attempted a night attack. By some accident, the Royalists realised how close the rebels were. A pistol was fired off. The watch gave the alarm. The camp rushed to arms and fell upon the little army. On July 6th 1685, at the Battle of Sedgemoor, which lasted perhaps for no more than an hour or two, the rebels became helpless targets for the royal guns.

The King's cavalry rode down from Weston Zoyland, and a portion of the rebels was put to flight. The untrained horses of Monmouth's army, unused to the flash and noise of musketry, took fright and scattered over the moors in all directions. His foot-soldiers, though many were only armed with the tools with which they tilled the ground fought valiantly until they were utterly cut to pieces, long after their leader in despair had fled for his life from the battlefield. The whole of the day was spent by the King's soldiers in chasing the fleeing rebels and in searching for their hiding places. By the evening, five hundred prisoners had been taken. They were all shut up in the church of Weston Zoyland. Some died there. Few of the rest escaped execution.

Disguised, Monmouth made his way as far as the New Forest, hoping to reach the coast to make his escape. A few days afterwards he was found hiding in a ditch, half buried in ferns and nettles, and nearly dead with hunger and fatigue. He was taken to London where he begged the King on his knees to have mercy on him and spare his life. James II had Monmouth found guilty of treason, beheaded on Tower Hill – it is said in a bungling manner.

The rebellion over, the King sent Judge Jeffreys, a harsh and cruel man, to Taunton, with four more judges under him, to try the rebels and punish them for daring to rise up against him. A most terrible time followed. Jeffreys showed neither justice nor mercy. His dealings with the rebels became known as the 'Bloody Assize.'

The precept to the Sheriff for the execution of rebels sets forth the ghastly details in full. These are:

Duke of Monmouth.

Judge Jeffreys.

By the King,
A PROCLAMATION.

JAMES R.

Whereas We have received Certain Information, That James Duke of Monmouth, Ford late Lord Gray Outlawed for High Treason, with divers other Traytors and Outlaws, are lately Landed in an Hostile manner at Lyme, in Our County of Dorset, And have Possessed themselves of Our said Town of Lyme. And have sent and dispersed some of their Trayterous Complices into the Neighbouring Countreys to Incite them to Joyn in open Rebellion against Us.

We do hereby, with the Advice of Our Privy Council, Declare and Publish the said James Duke of Monmouth, and all his Complices, Adherents, Abettors, and Advisers, Traytors and Rebells; And do Command and Require all Our Lieutenants, Deputy-Lieutenants, Sheriffs, Justices of the Peace, Mayors, Bayliffs, and all other Our Officers Civil and Military, to use their utmost endeavours to Seize and Apprehend the said James Duke of Monmouth, Ford late Lord Gray, and all their said Confederates and Adherents; And all and every other Person and Persons that shall be Aiding or Abetting the aforesaid Traitors and Rebells: And the said Persons and every of them to Secure until Our further Pleasure be known, as they will Answer the contrary at their utmost peril.

Given at Our Court at *Whitehall* this Thirteenth day of *June*, 1685. And in the First Year of Our Reign.

God save the King.

LONDON, Printed by the Assigns of *John Bill* deceas'd: And by *Henry Hills*, and *Thomas Newcomb*, Printers to the Kings Most Excellent Majesty, 1685.

Declaration.

> ... to will and require of you on sight hereof to erect a gallows in the most public place to hang the said traitors on, and that you provide halters to hang them with, and a sufficient number of faggots to burn the bowells, and a furnace or cauldron to boil their heads and quarters, and salt to boil them with, half a bushell to each traitor, and tar to tar them with, and a sufficient number of spears and poles to fix and place their heads and quarters, and that you warn the owners of four oxen to be ready with drag and wain ... and you with a guard of 40 able-men at the least to be present at 8am of the morning to be assisting me or my deputy.

Three men, not necessarily natives of the borough, were executed at Langport, being victims of the Bloody Assize in September, and having appeared in Court to face the infamous Chief Justice Jeffreys, who bullied his wretched prisoners, laughed at their sufferings and showed mercy to none. Humphrey Pierce, Nicholas Venting and John Selewood were hung and quartered. It is said three hundred people were hanged, and eight hundred and forty more sent away from their homes to work as slaves in the West Indies. Hundreds more were flogged, fined or imprisoned. The brutal Judge even ordered an aged lady, Alicia Lisle, to be put to death because she had sheltered fugitives after the battle. Another poor woman, Mrs. Gaunt, was burnt alive for the same reason. The hard-hearted King, instead of reproving Jeffreys for his brutality, actually made him Lord Chancellor, as a reward for what he had done!

The completeness of his victory made James feel secure, but the people's hate for their King grew. Even his soldiers became faithless. William of Orange, the King's Dutch nephew, was invited to come to England with an army to end James' misrule. James at once marched against William when he landed at Torbay, November 5th 1688, but this time soldiers deserted. The King escaped capture by hurrying back to London. Fearing for his own safety if he fell into the hands of his enraged subjects, James sent his wife and child to France. Twenty four hours later, the King followed them, taking with him the Great Seal, which he dropped into the Thames, hoping to make things as difficult as possible for the Government. The Seal, curiously enough, was found a few days later, and James too was discovered by sailors and sent back to London, rather to the disgust of William, anxious to be rid of him. No-one hindered James when he tried a second time to escape later, and he managed to reach France safely.

The Crown was offered to William and Mary, his wife, who were to rule as joint sovereigns. William would direct the government. William and Mary both promised to govern according to rules laid down by the Convention which were made into an Act of Parliament, known as the Bill of Rights. The Convention was an assembly of members of the House of Lords and representatives of the Commons. This change in the government was called the Revolution. It marked the beginning of another new period in English history. From that time, no-one has been able to pretend that the Kings of England rule, except by the authority of Parliament.

A plot was discovered in 1696 to assassinate William II (1689-1702) and a wave of loyalty spread throughout the land. William and Mary were a great contrast to each other. William was a thin delicate-looking man, quiet and reserved, while Mary, tall and stately, was bright and talkative – much more the most popular. The King, his mind full of the difficulties of ruling justly the people under his care, was neither understood nor loved by his subjects, but Mary, with her simple piety and generosity, soon won both their affection and admiration. The two sovereigns reigned most happily together. As long as Mary lived, her popularity was a great safeguard to the King, but in 1694, she died of smallpox, to the great grief of her husband and the whole nation. From the time of her death, William's life was in constant danger from the followers of James II, who made plot after plot to kill him.

A document was issued to strengthen William's position, which declared William 'rightful and lawful King', and besides Viscount Hardinge, Lord of Langport manor, Stowell of Low Ham, Sir E. Phelps, the Recorder, and the Portreeve and Burgesses, the rest of the inhabitants of the town and borough of Langport Eastover signed the oath roll. To quote

> ... Whereas there have been an horrid and detestable conspiracy formed and carried on by papistes and other wicked and traitorous persons for assassinating His Majesty's royal person in order to encourage an invasion from France and subvert our Religion Laws and Liberties, wee whose names are herein subscribed doe heartily sincerely and solemnly professe, testify and declare that His Majesty King William is rightful and

lawful King of these realms, and wee doe mutually promise and engage to stand by and assist each other to the uttermost of our power in the support and defence of His Majesty's most sacred person and Government against the late King James and all his adherents.

They further undertook to avenge his death if he was murdered and to support the succession of Anne (the second daughter of James II). The signatories included Robert Puddy (Portreeve), Burgesses: Ambrose Budd, John Michell, Hugh Caselman, W. Ball, Th. Hannam, W. Browning and J. Hartland; Town Clerk: J. Isham; Sergeant-at-Mace: John Ffido. Sixty other names followed, including James Hurd, George Paviour, George Stuckey, W. Hartland, R. Burrowes, T. Millard, E. Culliford, T. Brimble, W. Ash, T. Webb, B. Crosses, R. West, Vincent Boldy, J. Bush, G. Sawtell, B. Viney, J. Ball, W. Lye, D. Thomas, J. White, W. Treasure, J. Glover, J. Denham, J. Savage, J. Lang, Quirke, Larcomb, Bishop, Coggin, Hurtnole, Crossman, Gould and Saunders.

To continue with the history of Langport Manor, Viscount Hardinge's estates being encumbered with heavy mortgages, the manor itself was sold to the principal creditor in 1698, Sir William Brownlowe, whose son sold it in 1717 to William, the fourth Lord Berkeley of Straton. Lord Berkeley's will (he died in 1741) said that the manor was to be divided between his four daughters. The two quarter shares held by Ann and Jane (who both died unmarried before their father) passed to their brother John, Lord Berkeley, who died in 1773. The quarter share held by Frances was left to her son, William, Lord Byron, who sold it to Stamp Brooksbank in 1760, and the fourth share, held by Barbara, passed on her death in 1772 to a Dr. John Bettesworth.

In 1777, all four shares were purchased by Henry Hoare. On his death they passed to his daughter Anne, wife of her cousin Sir Richard Hoare, and eventually to their son, Sir Richard Colt Hoare. Sir Richard sold the manor to Uriah and George Messiter for £150 in 1808, who conveyed it in the following year to Langport Corporation for £250. The Corporation held the manor until the borough was dissolved in 1886. Thereafter, it was retained by Langport Town Trust, whose members since 1966 have been appointed by Langport Parish Council.

Chapter 15

Langport School - Schoolmasters - Langport Corporation - Queen Anne - Coronation Day Celebrations - George I - George II - George III - Parish History - Social Life.

From 1706 when the Court appointed the Grammar School Trustees, Minutes were regularly kept of school business. The Corporation continued to give generous support and appears to have given the schoolmaster, Henry Norman, the use of the Hanging Chapel as a School House. He was paid a salary of £20 per annum, increased later to £22. When he died in 1730, his son of the same name, was appointed to the school with a salary of about £29 per annum. In 1742, the Trustees deprived son Henry of his office on the grounds he had violated the rules of the school about religious training and worship on schooldays and Sundays '... that he neglected to teach, and had been absent from the school without permission of the Governors ...'

The next schoolmaster appointed was William Hart, who received about £24 per annum. The Trustees sent him gifts like the following: 'Half a pig weighing 119lbs ... £1 7s.3d.' and 'Cheese, Butter and Pork £4 ...' He died in 1784 aged seventy-two years, having resigned ten years previously on condition his son Henry succeeded him. The salary of Henry Hart at times only amounted to £13 per annum. On this poor salary he proved to be a very poor schoolmaster. The Trustees appointed a J. Brown as his assistant, but J. Brown did not take up the post.

Langport Corporation drew up a petition against poor Henry Hart, who was deposed by the Trustees, as he had not replied to charges against him. Mr. W. Moore was elected in his place, but the latter resigned a few months later because Mr. Hart refused to give up the school, and defied two notices of ejection from the Hanging Chapel served on him. He in turn prosecuted the steward of the Governors for not paying his salary. Later in the year, they all came to terms and on receipt of a sum of £41, Henry Hart signed a release to the Trustees from any further demands.

In 1790, Mr. Quekett was appointed. He moved the school to a good substantial brick house in Bow Street, of the Queen Anne style, where he was Headmaster for fifty-two years.

The Corporation's Minute Book shows instances of discipline applied to its members. William Browning was deposed and removed from the committee for irregular behaviour as Portreeve. Mr. Alsop and Mr. Brice were discharged for not attending and for living out-of-town. Mr. T. Beedall, Portreeve, failed in his business as a boat owner and was removed from his office in 1762. Both W. Hart and J. Ash were expelled for misbehaviour.

If poor Mr. Beedall's notebook is any indication, his financial ruin made him a rather morbid man, forever concerned about his digestion, his insomnia and the apples in his orchard. His concern for his daughters made him reluctant to let them see plays at the Town Hall, but two highlights of his life were recorded in great detail. In 1768 he rode over to Dillington House in the hope of obtaining some employment from the Prime Minister, Lord North. He only received a dinner with the head servants – but what a dinner!

> Dish of fish, a sirloin of beef roasted, a loin of veal with cauliflower, carrots, etc., for the first course, and for the second, a roast turkey, a hare, pigeon pie, fried oysters, chicken tarts, laver, etc. Drank water at dinner, after dinner four glasses of port wine.

He did not sleep too well that night!

He and his wife went to Bath and took a room for three months for £3, but the romantic balls and card parties were not for him. Mr. Beedall was much happier worrying about the floods in his orchard in Langport.

William II, who had founded another British Institution, the National Debt, by borrowing £1.2m at eight per cent from the newly created Bank of England in 1694, died after a fall from his horse, and Parliament passed an Act in 1702 to ensure that his sister-in-law, Queen Anne, could not dispose of Crown lands freely. William had made considerable grants of lands to his supporters.

On Queen Anne's Coronation Day, Langport Corporation spent £3 12s.6d. at the Swan on ale for the people, but when Anne died and her son George I became King, it spent almost no money. George was a short, heavy-looking man, untidy in dress, with awkward manners. he spoke no English, and very little French, having spent all his life in Hanover. In Langport, his Coronation aroused no enthusiasm, he having been '... made in Germany ...', but when George II came to the throne in 1727, Langport was determined to be jolly.

At the Black Swan 10s.6d. was spent: at the Five Bells another 10s.6d.; 14s.0d. on gunpowder; 5s.0d. on bell-ringers; and £4.2s.6d. on other celebrations. George II, a small, plain man, forty-four-years-old, was faithful to his friends and those who served him. Robert Walpole continued as Chief Minister and as long as he had his own way, the country was peaceful for it was kept carefully out of all European wars. Large sums too were spent on George III's Coronation in 1761 – on illuminations at the Town Hall, and on celebrations when he recovered from illhealth. George and Queen Charlotte had fifteen children, thirteen of whom reach maturity. The eldest was George IV, King in 1820, the year his father died, blind and insane.

In 1678 (in Charles II's reign), an Act was passed requiring burial in woollen, which proposed to discourage the importation of linen and encourage home manufacture of wool. An affidavit of burial in woollen was given to the incumbent, with a penalty payable of £5, for any violation of the Act. The fine was paid by any of the wealthy who could not endure the thought of woollen garments. The export of wool was forbidden from 1660-1825, so large areas of land became pasture for the production of the raw material. Pressure on the limited agricultural land around Langport was great, as a result of which in 1772 it was stated the town 'being unable to supply itself, is obliged to purchase provisions at an exorbitant rate'. A somewhat different situation to that of the early 11th century when Langport was almost self-sufficient.

The medieval textile trade continued into the late seventeenth century when cloth-workers and worsted-combers were mentioned, and later feltmaking. A glover was recorded in 1788 and gloving was carried on at Ensor House in Bow Street until 1971. Other occupations in the town during the eighteenth century included tobacconist, apothecary, tobaccotong maker, nail-maker, peruke-maker, soap-boiler and hairdresser. There were two auctioneers, six lawyers, two printers and book-binders, and umbrella manufacturer, and a watch-maker. In 1830 a land and timbersurveyor was mentioned, a boat-builder, an engineer, and a soap and candle manufacturer in 1840. By 1859 there was a brightsmith and bellhanger, a cheese factory, three jewellers, two undertakers, and later still, three builders and a photographer.

A glimpse of social life in the eighteenth century is provided by an advertisement in the *Sherborne Mercury*, stating a purse of two guineas would be played for at sword and dagger on Thursday, June 16th 1768. On the Friday there would be backsword (made of wood) play for one guinea and in the afternoon, play with sword and dagger for one guinea more. There would be dinner on the table at 1pm each day – all at the White Horse, Langport. Other pastimes included cracking crowns with single stick and quarter staff: bull, bear and badger baiting: cock fighting: pugilism 'til smothered in blood' and duelling.

People of quality liked to attend hangings at the infamous Ilchester Gaol, on Hang Fair Days. Crowds attended from parishes around, and danced and drank at the alehouses. In the eighteenth century spirits could be obtained everywhere at small cost. Drunkenness became a national vice. Human life continued to be of little value. Children were sentenced for life, or hung. Until 1825 hanging was literally awarded for nearly every offence. The last Hang Fair Day was said to have been in 1835 when the two murderers of John Harvey of Langport were hanged at a field called Gallows Five Acres.

Primary School, Langport.

Although clever and talented, George IV attracted neither the love nor the respect of his people. Trade was bad as the use of machinery instead of hand labour threw many out of work, and the price of bread was high. But Robert Peel, leader of the House of Commons, did much to improve the condition of the country. He altered laws relating to punishment, which had always been terribly severe, and thereafter, the death sentence was only passed for murder and a few other serious offences, and a new police force was formed for London. In 1829 a Bill was passed which gave Catholics the same rights as the Protestants. Thanks to the King's good ministers, the reign was a time of real progress.

The first year of William IV's reign (1830-1837) was the beginning of a great change in everyone's life. In that year a railway between Manchester and Liverpool, planned by George Stephenson, was opened. At the same time steamships increased the speed that people could travel by sea. Trade increased in all directions. Coal was wanted to work steam-engines, so manufacturers went where coal was abundant. People left the south, and the old towns became smaller and less important. In 1833 the slavery trade was stopped for ever. William died after a useful seven years' reign, and Victoria at eighteen years, the daughter of his younger brother, succeeded to the throne.

The years 1750-1850 became the years of Langport's greatest prosperity.

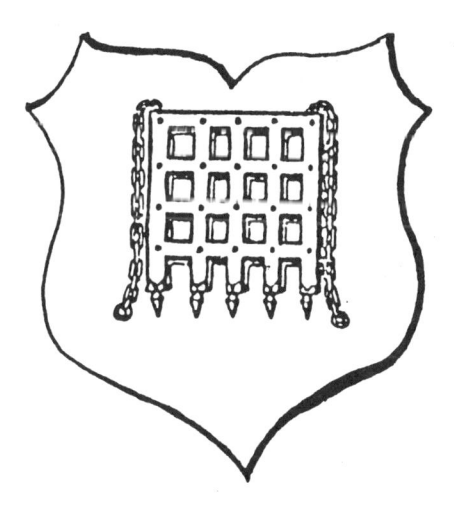

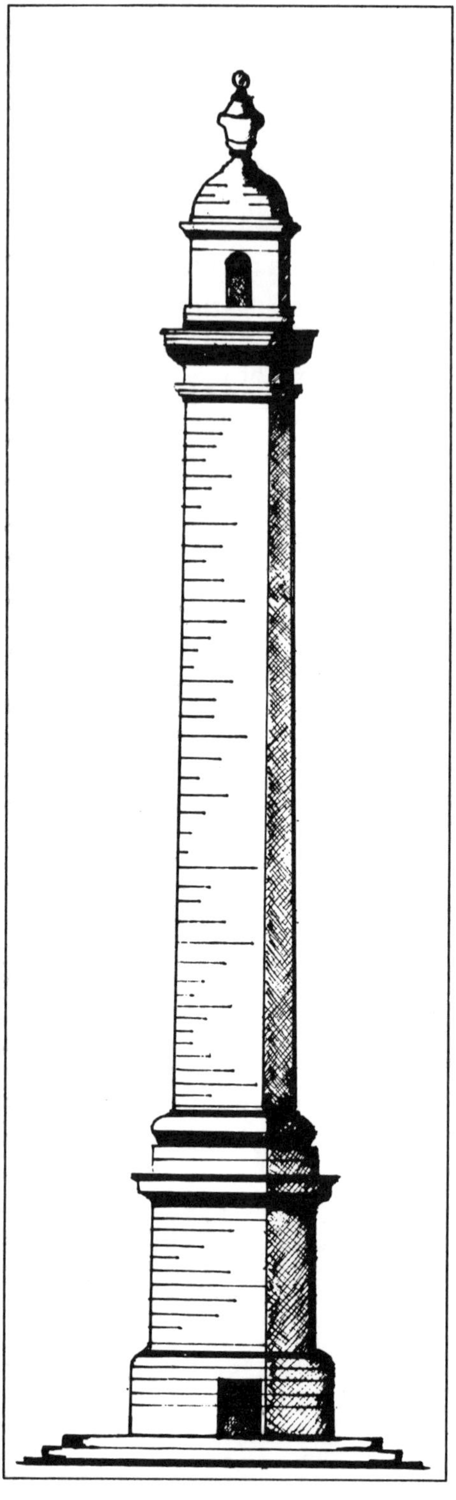

Chapter 16

Years of Langport's Greatest Prosperity - William Pitt, the Elder - Pynsent Monument - Stuckey's Bank - Stuckey/Bagehot Partnership - Walter Bagehot - River Trade Flourishing - Lovibond's Railway.

In 1766, Wm. Pitt the Elder, first Earl of Chatham, gave £5. 5s. 'to raise ye gard walls of Broad Bo.' About this time he was building a monument from a design by Capability Brown, to the memory of the eccentric Sir William Pynsent, who had willed him his estate in Curry Rivel. It was later alleged he had wanted to thank Pitt for his opposition to a proposed cider tax. Pitt (Prime Minister) had many devices to get money in that period of the war with France and all the ingenuity of financiers was invoked to discover new sources of taxation. Taxes (it has been said) were imposed on everything which enters into the mouth, or covers the body, on everything pleasant to see, hear, feel, smell, or taste, everything on earth or under the earth, everything which came from abroad or was grown at home.

Pitt wrote of idyllic days spent at Burton Pynsent. It was said to have been a great sight to see him driving in a coach and six with ten outriders. Lady Chatham wrote of meeting her son, Pitt the Younger, in the High Street (Bow Street), Langport, '... a street which for the future I shall visit with far greater pleasure than if its walls were built by Palladio and consecrated by ancient fame.'

The same Lady Chatham was responsible for dissuading the lord of the manor in 1791 from letting his stretch of the River Parrett to a firm of fishmongers whom she claimed would clear it of fish. The conflicting jurisdictions over the river of both manor and borough were evidently reconciled with the selling of the manor to Langport Corporation in 1809.

The Pitts were not able to enjoy Burton Pynsent for long. Lady Chatham died in 1803, and the estate was sold, mainly because of Pitt the Elder's

---

Opposite: Burton Pynsent Monument.

extravagance. Lord Chatham had built a wing on his great mansion which, when the rest of the building was pulled down for its material by the creditors, happily remained. The property was bought by Wm. Pinney, M.P. and later inherited by Charles Pinney, married to Vincent Stuckey's daughter.

There is little doubt that Langport's prosperity in the late eighteenth and nineteenth centuries depended principally on the trading firm of Stuckey and Bagehot. Grandfather George Stuckey, a worsted comber then sergemaker, came to Langport in the late seventeenth century from Kingsdon, taking lease of a house in Up Streete. His son, father George Stuckey, was a merchant who went into partnership with Thomas Bagehot, maltster, who took a lease of other premises in Up Street, including part of Hill House, with brewery and malthouse. Together they traded in a wide range of goods.

The ability of the Stuckey-Bagehot firm in Langport caused a large increase in the population. Abundant harvests between 1715 and 1765 led to large exports of corn, which with stone, brick, tile, timber, coal, iron and salt formed the basis of River Parrett commerce. Charges were made on all vehicles unloading at both Great and Little Bow bridges, and on carts travelling over them. The Corporation took to law anyone trying to evade them. Defoe and Richardson, writers travelling through Britain in 1769, remarked that Langport was a well-frequented market town on the River Parrett, navigable for barges to Bridgwater, and having a good trade in lead, oil, wine, hemp, flax, pitch, tar, dye stuffs, etc. By 1793, the partnership was carrying on trade with Birmingham, Manchester, Liverpool and London, both by road and water. The Ilchester Canal Co. improved the waterways around the town, by deepening and straightening the Portlake Rhine, later known as the Catchwater. Two Acts obtained resulted in the formation of the Parrett Navigation Co., which operated until 1878.

Giving evidence to the House-of-Commons Committee on the Parrett Navigation Co. in 1836, Henry Price, a civil engineer, reported that 'there is at present an overfall at Langport Bridge presenting an absolute barrier to any barges passing during times of floods thus rendering it necessary to shift the cargoes on men's shoulders to small barges above the bridge.' This overfall was stated by the promoters to be two-feet six-inches, although James Warren, who had been instructed to take levels along the river bed, reckoned the rise over the sill to be one foot.

Above: Langport's ancient bridge;
Below: Great Bow Bridge, erected 1840.

The Company did more again for Langport's waterborne traffic. It improved navigation and built locks up to Thorney. It created a little port at Westport by cutting a branch canal to meet the Parrett's tributary, the Isle, shortly before it joins the main stream in its passage past Muchelney to Langport.

By agreement with the Corporation, the P.N.C. pulled down the old Bow Bridge (described as a narrow, dilapidated medieval structure of about nine spans) in 1840, and erected the present one of three limestone arches. Before that, coal or other goods had been taken out of barges, put into withy baskets, and then carried through the bridge upon a plank into two small boats above. Two men, one horse, one boy and the two boats took half the load on to Thorney where it was discharged. But most of the time two smaller boats could not carry as much as the large one, and sometimes had to lie about in the river for a day or two. In future, with the use of only one boat and one horse, there would be a great saving. Part of the agreement was that the P.N.C. would pay for its maintenance and the Corporation £500 towards the cost.

A few years earlier, Henry Lovibond, a carrier in Langport, had tried to overcome the problems caused by difference in the river's levels and was given permission to remove stone pitching under one of the arches 'to enable the boats the better to pass, there being another bed of pitching under it', and then to lay a railway or tram road under the bridge for the purpose of taking boats from the pool to the level above in the times of scarcity of water. Lovibond's Railway! That the latter contraption was built is shown by receipts for compensation paid by the P.N.C. when it was later removed.

Much merchandise was distributed from Langport wharves. A queue of carts could have been seen in the early morning stretching from the top to the bottom of Bow Street, waiting to be loaded. At one time it is said twenty captains lived in the town, and boys applied to be taken on as apprentices for the Stuckey-Bagehot shipping line. The firm owned fourteen East Indiamen, as well as nineteen river barges. Their square riggers bore timber from Canada, the loads being discharged at Combwich. They owned the fully-rigged American built 'British Empire' which at 1347 tons was the largest vessel to be registered at Bridgwater. This probably intended for the timber trade, foundered in 1860. In 1847 a 66-ton ketch, the 'Thorney' was built at Langport and floated downstream to be fitted out for coasting, the size of the craft being restricted by successive Bridgwater bridges.

Father George Stuckey's younger son, Samuel, founded Stuckey's Bank in Langport in 1770, aided by his brother, George, but it was Samuel's nephew who showed a special genius for banking. Apparently nephew Vincent presented himself at Burton Pynsent to Lady Chatham, asking her to introduce him to the Prime Minister. He took her letter to London and obtained a clerkship in the Treasury, for a time being private secretary to Pitt himself.

The banking business had grown out of the freight trade. The many customers of Stuckey-Bagehot not wanting the responsibility of handling gold and silver, would lay it up with the firm and receive in return handwritten notes on vellum – both easier to carry and to pass on. In 1796 a run was made on the Banks in fear of a French invasion. But men trusted Stuckey as much as their own old stocking! A story is told of the Bank in its early days. Farmers were heard saying at Taunton and Bridgwater markets 'The bank be broke down to Langport.' The words were thought to refer to the banking business, but in truth the River Parrett had broken a part of its bank in flood-time. Not Stuckey's Bank! Family banks merged into Stuckey's Bank in 1826 which became one of the earliest joint stock banks in the country, with branches at Bridgwater and Bristol, later at Taunton and Wells. The Bank (said to have been where now stands the present branch of the National Westminster Bank) was taken over by Parr's Bank in 1909, later absorbed by the Westminster (National Westminster). At the time of the amalgamation, Stuckey's Bank had a banknote circulation second only to that of the Bank of England.

The elder Vincent Stuckey kept a pack of hounds in Whatley, and lived in patriarchal style, hospitable, freehanded and popular in Langport. He could have been seen at times seated under the great elm on the Hill, fronting the west door of the Church, near the family home at Hill House, chatting to his neighbours. He died in 1845. Mrs. Vincent Stuckey, with two daughters and no surviving son, adopted her eldest grandson as heir to her husband's property and to his position in the Bank. On her death, Vincent Wood changed his name to Stuckey, continuing to live at Hill House as he had done in his grandmother's lifetime. He possessed much of his grandfather's business acumen, and had a similar genial personality.

The Bagehot family could be traced back to the days of the Norman Conquest. Thomas Bagehot, a solicitor's son, had four children, Ann,

Above: Vincent Stuckey
Below: Hill House

Above: Walter Bagehot
Below: Hurd's Hill House.

Priscilla, Thomas Watson and Robert Codrington. The latter lived in an old house with mullion windows on the west side of the Parrett, which site was later occupied by Bradford's Yard. In 1826 Robert built his house at Hurd's Hill. The young Walter Bagehot was taken by his father, Thomas, to view the laying of the first stone. Thomas himself moved there from Bank House in Bow Street, where Walter was born, ten years later after Robert's death, taking with him not only his family but his mulberry tree.

Thomas Watson Bagehot was managing director and vice chairman of Stuckey's Bank for thirty years. He married Edith, described as a fascinating woman of great charm, elegance of figure, chatty and vivacious, who was son George Stuckey's daughter and Vincent's sister.

Walter Bagehot was born in 1826. Educated under Mr. Quekett at the Grammar School, a thoughtful boy, at the age of fourteen he wrote poetry. But for him, his uncle Vincent Stuckey's home was the centre of life. However quiet the town sometimes, its carters, wharf and barge population were about early. Mail coaches dashed in and drew up at the Langport Arms, and banker Stuckey drove in and around the town with his carriage and postilions.

Bagehot left Langport and went on to further education at Bristol, staying with his mother's brother-in-law, Dr. Pritchard, the ethnologist. He, in 1842, entered University College, London, and was called to the Bar ten years later. Instead of following that profession, however, he joined his father in the shipping and banking businesses at Langport, where he learned practical finance. His book *Lombard Street* was considered the most sensible and popular description of the banking world in those years.

The great work of Walter Bagehot's life was in finance. Lord Beaconsfield was guided by his advice in purchasing the Suez Canal shares. He was consulted by both Liberal and Conservative Chancellors of the Exchequer, and devised the simple, practicable and intelligible Treasury Bills we use today. Walter Bagehot too was an early advocate of the reform of the House of Lords by the introduction of men of worth as peers. The books which gave him his European reputation were *The English Constitution* and *Economic Studies*. He married a Miss Wilson, daughter of the first editor of the *Economist*, later becoming its editor. A vigorous and brilliant speaker on a wide range of subjects, he died of heart disease at the early age of fifty-one, and is buried in Langport churchyard.

Chapter 17

Education - Quekett Family - 1815 Celebrations - Fishing - Markets - Amenities in Langport.

Chap-books were available in country places from the sixteenth to the nineteenth centuries, carried by chap-men or pedlars and sold for pence or exchanged for rags or other articles. In 1723 a chap-book published in three editions and sold for the author's benefit was entitled *A Brief and True Relation of the Surprising Case of Edward Millard of Langport, in the County of Somerset. Shewing the fearful Tragedy of his Life, and his hard conflict with the Powers of Darkness: wherein the Great Mercy and Power of God hath been manifested in a wonderful manner in succouring the Tempted and Despairing Soul. Recollected and written by Himself, and published for a Memorial to the Glory of God and the Benefit and Instruction of all those who may labour under the like Temptations. 2nd edition with large additions, wherein the causes of his Misery is more largely set forth.*

Education has been well catered for in Langport. There was a dame school kept by Sarah Hurtnell – perhaps a descendant of that Nicholas Hurtnell, who in 1604 obtained a licence to teach Latin in the town. And there were a number of others. Miss Norton kept a dame school on the upper floor of a building at the rear of what is now Langport Stores, but was Norton's Grocery Store. Elizabeth and Ann Lake ran a girls' boarding school, and records show there were two day schools in 1818, both probably private. The National School founded in 1827, followed by the Board School of 1876 in North Street, lay in Huish Parish, between The Beeches and Bond's Pool Lane. Pupils were expected to pay one penny per week for education there.

In 1790, the Rev. William Quekett, who originated from Scotland, became the highly respected master of the Grammar School. He taught all the youth of Langport and its neighbourhood, giving them a solid groundwork of general knowledge. Langport's Register records that at his funeral all the shops in the town were closed out of respect for his

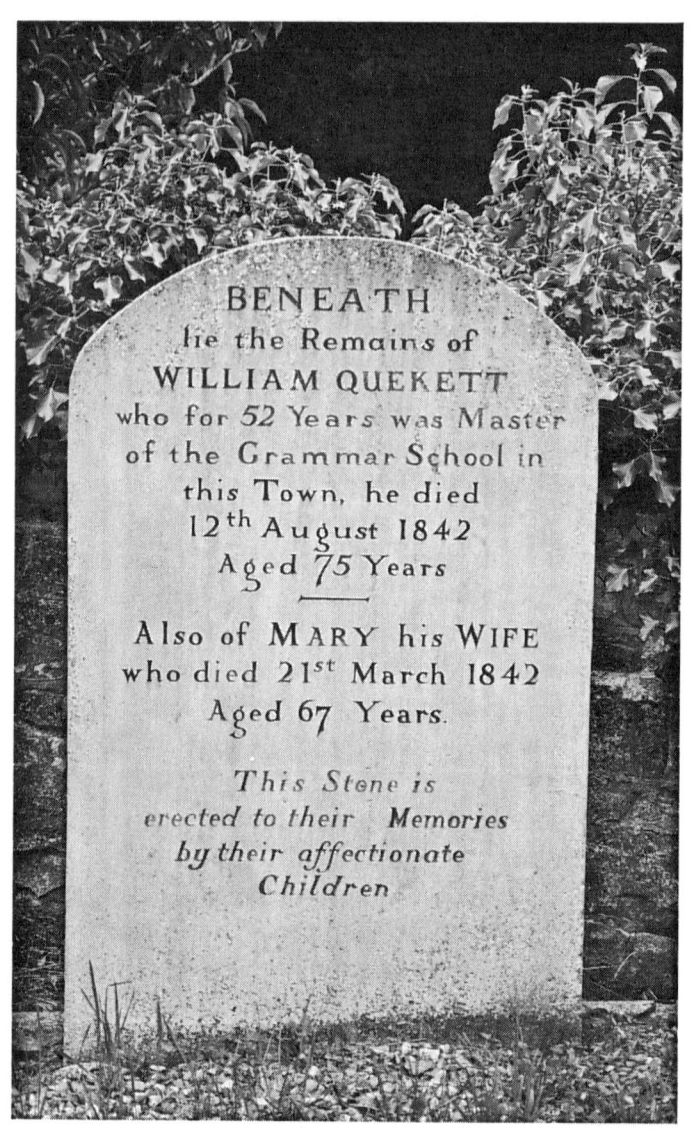

> BENEATH
> lie the Remains of
> WILLIAM QUEKETT
> who for 52 Years was Master
> of the Grammar School in
> this Town, he died
> 12th August 1842
> Aged 75 Years
>
> Also of MARY his WIFE
> who died 21st March 1842
> Aged 67 Years.
>
> This Stone is
> erected to their Memories
> by their affectionate
> Children

Rev. Queckett's grave.

memory. The pall-bearers were all old pupils, including Walter Bagehot, as were the ringers, who rang a muffled peal. Wm. Quekett brought with him to Langport that love of poetry seen in some of his pupils. He himself wrote:

> In the summer months the moor appears as with snow. This appearance is caused by the immense flocks of geese which are fed there chiefly for the sake of the feathers and quills. One goosier will own as many as 3000 geese. Every year the poor creatures are plucked as closely as a cook would pluck them before roasting.

William Quekett, Jnr., wrote in his *Reminiscences of My Life* of the celebrations after Napoleon's defeat in 1815 at the Battle of Waterloo.

> In Langport we had a splendid procession. Every trade was represented, and had something distinctive to mark its representatives. The tinmen wore tin hats: the glass-blowers carried specimens of their industry: the blacksmiths had a lorry on which a forge was set up. The huntsman walked in his red coat and black velvet cap, with two hounds on leashes ... then 'Peace' and 'Plenty' were represented. 'Peace' was characterized by a young lady – a very handsome girl – ... who led a pet lamb. A man of the name of Tom Mabey and fat Mrs. Denham represented John Bull and his wife. They carried a huge round of beef and a plum-pudding on a butler's tray – the symbol of 'Plenty'.
>
> ... The whole procession made its way to the Parish Church, where a sermon was preached ... from Church all adjourned to the moor for dinner, which was well prepared and sumptuous and substantial. After a plentiful repast the company, rich and poor, joined in games, which lasted until evening, when all adjourned to the town. Here there was a ball in the Market Hall ... the Portreeve opened the ball with Mrs. Ewens, the pastry-cook. There were illuminations throughout the town, and a grand display of fireworks ... the feasting lasted for three days: the rejoicings filled the souls of us youngsters with immense reverence for the greatness of the Duke of Wellington.

The young Quekett wrote on Hunting and Shooting:

> The old parson gave us a hunt every Saturday afternoon when a hare was found. ... Surrounding the town, and indeed as boundaries between the large fields and sections of moorlands, were wide ditches, some of them almost deep enough for canals. We were all taught to jump these sometimes of the width of 14ft. In the wintertime, these afforded us good skating ... to jump them a "poord" was used - a pole with a flat wooden foot, which prevents its sinking into the mud at the bottom of the ditch. When out snipe-shooting we generally went two together: one carried the gun and the other the 'poord'. He who by duty or inclination carried the gun, had the base of the 'poord' fixed by his companion in the middle of the ditch: and it was an act of dexterity for the gun-bearer to swing himself across safely, and to transfer the pole to his companion, so that he too might take the leap and drag the 'poord' out for further use.

and on Carp Fishing:

> The River Parrett contains great quantities of other fish - roach, dace, perch, tench, and carp. I have caught roach 2lbs in weight. But probably the most interesting fishing is that for carp. Carp could never be taken by angling except at one period of the year when the blackberries are perfectly ripe. For their capture we generally used casting-nets which we, as boys, made ourselves.
>
> There was an old clergyman in the neighbourhood whose house stood on the site of an old monastery, surrounded by a moat. In this moat were very fine carp of as much as 10 to 12lbs. in weight. Overhanging the moat were some large blackberry bushes ... when the time came, we repaired with rod and line to Mr. Mends' moat at Aller, and there, baiting with a large ripe blackberry, we allowed the line to fall into the water just below one of the bushes. The bait was immediately taken, and we hooked a splendid carp. But we never could catch more than one the same day: for of all fish the carp are the most suspicious and timid.

All the Quekett sons, born and educated in the town, attained a certain renown after leaving it. William became Rector of Warrington. He wrote *What a London Curate can do if he tries* and founded the Female Emigration Society in 1849, with the co-operation of Sidney Herbert. John Thomas at sixteen years gave lectures in microscopical subjects, and spent most of his life at the College of Surgeons occupied with histology. Edwin was the virtual founder of the Royal Microscopical Society, a lecturer on botany and a fellow of the Linnean Society. His name is commemorated in the Brazilian genus of orchids, Quekettia, and Edward was an ornithologist, a banker in Langport and occasional portreeve. The Corporation let him house his valuable collection of stuffed birds in the Hanging Chapel, which was a museum until 1875.

Langport's flooded Streets.

In the early nineteenth century, Langport was constantly flooded, owing to the increase of drainage in the lands above. Water reached the tops of hedges – an annual event. Inhabitants took their pigs and fowls up into the bedroom. Boats rowed up and down the street to supply food. Their home being in Bow Street, the Quekett boys could keep a boat moored in their garden, and float up and down around the River Parrett capturing whatever was curious in the water, or unusual on land. Hence the museum housed many specimens of local plant life, and items of antiquity such as pottery and Roman remains discovered when the Corporation made a sewer from the Hill to Bow Street, as well as stuffed birds.

The Independents rented premises in 1807, but their efforts within the town initially met with little success. James Moreton, Independent minister, instigated the building of the present chapel on the North side of Bow Street and it was opened in 1829. The site, originally a withy bed, was bought from Vincent Stuckey, who objected to the chapel being built in Priest Lane near his home. The United Reformed Church is the result of a merger of the Congregationalists, the Presbyterians, and other smaller denominations. In 1883 it housed a Sunday School, and at the same time in the town there were three private boarding schools, and the master of the Grammar School was taking private pupils.

In 1903 nuns of the Order of Christian Instruction came to Langport to escape political pressures in France. They acquired and settled at Hill House, which they renamed St. Gilda's Convent, and where they established a girls' school. Today, after the school's closure, it is a Retreat and Conference Centre. Age Concern use it for their activities three days a week.

A house 'commonly called the town hall', standing on the site of the present building in Cheapside, was mentioned in 1596 – probably erected after Langport obtained its 1463 Charter. The present town hall, with market area beneath, was built in 1732 with a loan from the then portreeve. Two pairs of iron gates were set up in 1753, replaced by three pairs surmounted by a portcullis in 1840. Since 1967 it has been leased to the British Legion.

In 1840, the Registry Office was built on steel girders over the catchwater which still runs under it and under the road at Little Bow Bridge, although most of it was filled in in 1968. Some records show the two arches of that bridge were made into one about 1800, when Portlake Rhine was straightened and deepened – the Corporation paying £87 towards the cost.

From about 1855 Langport had a pig market on the south side of Cheapside. It was common for seven or eight hundred pigs to be on sale, but this area became a car park in 1937. A cattle market was held in the roadway in North Street until land at the north end of the street was given to the Town Trust by James Broadmead. The cattle market was discontinued after the Second World War. A weekly corn market was held under the Town Hall. There was another market for horses early in the 1900s.

*Above: Langport's Town Hall;
Below: Old Bow Street.*

Whatley, used for fairs in earlier times, had a sheep market.

Water has always been plentiful in Langport. Many houses in the town had their own pumps by the last century. Gas works were erected in Whatley when the Langport Coal Gas Company was formed in 1835. The town was first lit by electricity in 1932. Nowadays the Fire Brigade based at Somerton serves the parish, but in 1768 Langport maintained its own fire engine, drawn by horses, worked by hand, with leather buckets. It was kept in the church and neighbouring parishes had the use of it, paying £1 per annum, if they fetched and returned it. The Corporation acquired a new fire engine in 1845. A shed in the old pig market housed it until about 1877, when it was transferred to the Town Hall. Before that, for a time the engine stood in a shed in the Hanging Chapel garden.

New sewers were built for Langport in the mid-20s. Previously, Langport locks were closed to raise the water level above the town so that the nine culverts under Bow Street could be flushed and sewage carried firstly into North Street ditch, and finally back into the river north of the railway.

In 1793, there was a music club, then the Langport Literary and Scientific Association, and the Langport and District Rifle Club, which won the Daily Mail Cup in 1910 as first in the British Isles and second in the Empire. The Langport Friendly Society, which still meets annually, was revived in 1902 and in 1960.

1833 marked the year a nightwatch was appointed for the better protection of the town, and in 1837 a pair of stocks was made – burnt by a caretaker in 1906. Responsibility for the jail passed to the county authorities in 1878. A cottage was purchased in Whatley, and cells with stone ceilings and grills erected, with a resident police constable. At one time the sergeant-at-mace was entitled to six pence nightly for each prisoner. Today the police station at Somerton also serves Langport.

A cemetery and mortuary chapel were established for the benefit of Langport in 1880, the site in Huish being provided once more by James Broadmead.

Bow Street, 1994.

Chapter 18

Finances - The Coming of the Railway - Decline of Waterborne Traffic - Langport a Borough no longer - The Future

Towards the end of the eighteenth century, the Portreeve's accounts had frequently shown a deficit. Sir Richard Colt Hoare, lord of the manor, and the Corporation, having taken legal advice and conducted a new survey, sold many properties in the lower part of the town. The manor of Langport Eastover was bought, and the common grazing rights appertaining to it were sold. Many new houses were built, and the Corporation's profits were reinvested both in land in Westonzoyland and in purchasing securities in the Langport, Somerton and Castle Cary Turnpike Trust. Unhappily, those bonds fell considerably in value and when sold, fetched only three-quarters of their original cost.

The area at the top of the Hill became the most fashionable part of the town, with several substantial houses and large gardens. By this time, the greater part of Bow Street had been improved, and new buildings were demolished to make way for the widening of both Bow and North Streets. The town began to take on a very different look.

Tightly packed tenements along both sides of Bow Street with long narrow rear yards running at right angles to the road, had probably been the last to be laid out, after available frontages on the Hill had been occupied. The tenements were originally built for the burgesses, each one facing Bow Street – one width for the house side by side with an equal width for a cart or carriage. The only way to enlarge these houses in later years was to build on to the back; perhaps extend sideways into the archway; and then still later to re-design the enlarged dwelling at right angles to the road, e.g. Virginia House, said to have been an Elizabethan dwelling at one time built to face the street.

It has been written that about sixty years ago, there were terraces comprising in total about forty dwellings, in Langport, known as 'courts', *e.g.* Knight's Court, alongside the Dolphin, which is now Moor Park. Entry was by a very long and narrow passage leading in that case, direct to the backwater. The 'court' comprised three or four cottages with a small yard in front. The small cottages were at the rear of a larger dwelling facing Bow Street, and were for apprentices. Mr. Knight himself had a grocery business in the larger house. What is now Pocock's Yard was a 'court'. Beard's Yard could have been a 'court', named after James Beard, who owned a foundry, and Webb's Yard was probably a 'court' at one time. Phineas Winter Webb started a bakery there in 1894.

Webb's Bakery.

More recently, with most of the suitable building land in the parish already occupied, the town has been forced to expand north and northeast into Huish parish, where many of the district council houses lie. Garden City, part of which is on the site of the former Langport field, was begun in 1919, and the old people's bungalows on the former Memorial playing field were completed in 1963.

Modern private building within the parish has been mainly restricted to the southern slopes of Langport Hill, called St. Gilda's Close, and to sites on the western slope east of the old grammar school, now a private house. South of Cheapside the car park laid out in 1937 was extended in 1970, and recently further extended, principally to cater for visitors to Cocklemoor Park. A terrace of shops has been built nearby.

LANGPORT

The opening of Langport Railway Station (later Langport West Station) in 1853, was received with great enthusiasm in the town. Trains ran from Yeovil and attracted many passengers. The Bristol and Exeter Timetable announced: 'An omnibus meets every train. Post horses, carriages, etc. may be had at the Langport Arms and Dolphin Hotels.' As well as normal services, there were weekly market trains serving the area. The station closed to passenger traffic in 1964.

Langport East Station on the new London, Castle Cary and Taunton branch of the main West-of-England line (then the G.W.R.) was opened in 1906 and demolished years later. Foundations had to be dug to a depth of fifty feet or more over the red marl for the viaduct constructed over North Street moor. As it was found necessary to use some of the commoners' land, an 'exchange piece' was given in return.

The Railway Hotel with the longest bar in Langport was erected, with a cast-iron footbridge in two halves, giving access to the first floor from road level – the building is now divided into flats.

The Langport and Mid-Somerset Building Society appears to have been founded in 1859. A seed warehouse was recorded in 1875 and two garages and a jam factory by 1927. Industrial enterprises in the town in 1972 included two luggage manufacturers, a woodcraft firm, and Silkolene Lubricants. Until 1966 there was a seed processing and retailing firm, and the cheese factories near the foot of the Hill had in 1972 only recently closed down.

The *Langport and Somerset Herald* was established in 1855, thereafter recording the many and varied events affecting the town. In 1822, £4. 4s. was paid to the Portreeve to attend the House of Lords, and a Committee appointed to watch Lord Rosebery's Bill for the abolition of certain corporations. There was a petition of the town for a fresh Charter, but the Privy Council regretted it could not advise Her Majesty to grant it. On March 27th, 1886, it was stated that 'Langport a borough no longer ... a muffled peal on the bells of the fine old Church.'

But the coming of the railway resulted in the immediate decline of waterborne traffic. The Parrett Navigation Co. was taken over by the Somerset Drainage Commissioners. Of the earlier warehouses once used for goods brought up river, only one, a three-storeyed brick building remained – now restored. The last cargo passed under Bow Bridge in the 1940s. The population decreased from 1245 in 1831 to 686 in 1931. It stood at 777 in 1961.

Above: Langport West Station in flood;
Below: Looking towards Yeovil.

A 'court.'

Above: Viaduct;
Below: Langport Station.

By 1884 the treasurer's accounts showed a much increased deficit.

In 1887 the Charity Commission held an enquiry into the property of the former Corporation, and Langport Town Trust was founded to administer it and to liquidate the debts incurred by the dissolved corporation. The Trust appointed a steward and deputy-steward of the manor each year, and also a man to serve as hall-keeper and market bailiff. Lands earlier acquired in Westonzoyland were sold, as was the Langport Arms (the repair of which had been a constant drain on finances) and four cottages in Whatley. Having thus disposed of their assets and with no means of securing additional income to meet rising costs and liabilities, the trustees were unable to fulfil their obligations. Under these circumstances the parish council assumed control of the Trust in 1966.

The rule of the Corporation, the commonalty, the portreeves, on the whole had been wise, beneficial and dignified. They had given financial support to every project considered of benefit to the town. They had accepted responsibility for the bridges, the public buildings, the schools and the moors. They had noted every national and patriotic event of importance.

Langport is unique – unlike any other place in England - so what does the future hold for the town.

In November 1988, South Somerset District Council produced the draft of a Plan for the development of Langport and Somerton. To quote from the Introduction:

> Langport is one of the most interesting of South Somerset's many ancient settlements ... The great strength of character of the town reflects this trading role with a great variety of architectural styles and materials; and the remnants of warehousing and wharves ... today the town plays an important role for its many surrounding villages ... It has over 40 shops, several banks, hotels and hostelries and is a significant education centre. Cocklemoor is a vital town centre recreational asset, and the District Council will take a lead in its management and development ... A growth area of potential benefit to the town lies in pleasure boating ... Langport is defined as an Outstanding Heritage Settlement, for which an enhancement scheme is proposed ... Outside the town, the countryside is of high quality and forms part of a Special Landscape Area

... both parishes (Langport and Huish) lie in the Levels and Moors Landscape Improvement area.

Since the draft, Langport has gained a new Medical Centre, serving many other parishes in the neighbourhood, as well as a Youth Centre (Ridgway Hall) with parking, a much enlarged library is under construction, and there are plans to develop further the river area. The future could be good indeed. To quote T.S. Eliot:

Time present and Time past
Are both perhaps present in Time future,
And time future contained in Time past.

Old School House, 1994.

STEAM PRINTING WORKS,
NORTH STREET, LANGPORT.

THE LANGPORT HERALD,
PRICE ONE PENNY.
Established 1855.   Enlarged 1864.
FORTY COLUMNS.

TO ADVERTISERS.

The advantages of Advertising can hardly be overrated. Those who have most extensively adopted the system bear emphatic testimony to its value. Many tradesmen, who might otherwise have remained comparatively unknown and unnoticed, have by this means secured a large amount of patronage, and succeeded in establishing a thriving business. There is no other way of making public announcements that can compete in cheapness and efficiency with an Advertisement in a respectable, established Newspaper.

The Langport Herald, which is the only paper published within a circuit of 12 miles, and which has a wide circulation, will be found a most desirable medium.

TERMS FOR ADVERTISING.

	s.	d.
One to four lines	1	0
Five to ten lines	2	0
Twelve lines	2	6
Fifteen lines	3	0
Twenty lines	3	6
Twenty-five lines	4	0
Thirty lines	4	6

☞ Special Contracts for Advertisements inserted for Terms of Three, Six, and Twelve Months.

Orders for Advertisements sent by unknown correspondents should be accompanied with letter stamps or Post-Office order; if the latter, the order to be made payable to WALTER EDWARD BENNETT, Langport, Somerset.

Above: Advertisement from Kelly's Directory of Somerset, *1883.*
Below: The River Parrett in February 1940.

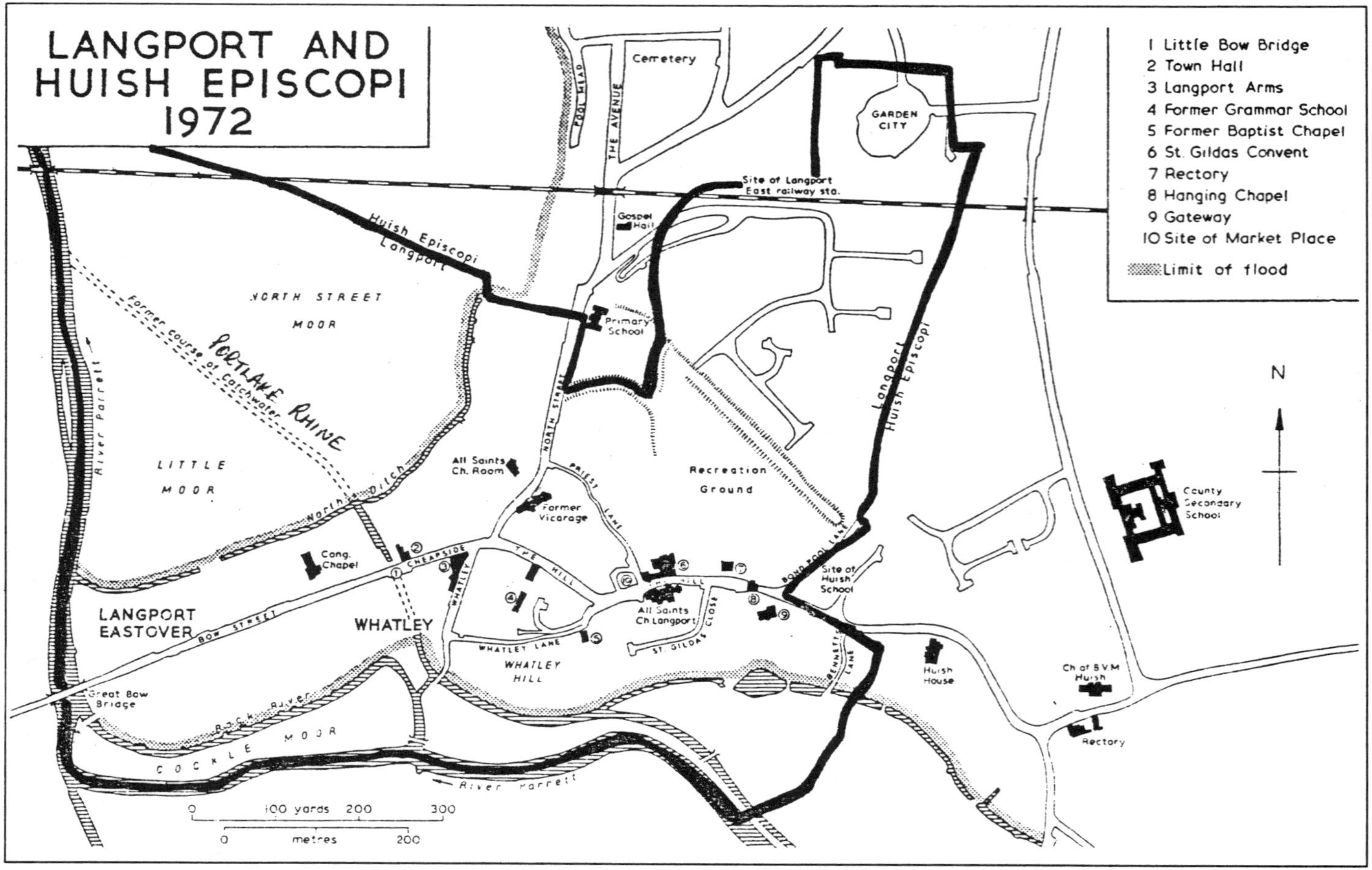
LANGPORT AND HUISH EPISCOPI 1972
1 Little Bow Bridge
2 Town Hall
3 Langport Arms
4 Former Grammar School
5 Former Baptist Chapel
6 St. Gildas Convent
7 Rectory
8 Hanging Chapel
9 Gateway
10 Site of Market Place
Limit of flood
N
Cemetery
POOL MEAD
THE AVENUE
GARDEN CITY
Site of Langport East railway sta.
Gospel Hall
Huish Episcopi
Langport
NORTH STREET MOOR
Former course of Catchwater
PORTLAKE RHINE
Primary School
NORTH STREET
Recreation Ground
LITTLE MOOR
River Parrett
North Ditch
All Saints Ch. Room
PRIEST LANE
Former Vicarage
County Secondary School
Cong. Chapel
CHEAPSIDE
THE HILL
BOND POOL LANE
Site of Huish School
All Saints Ch. Langport
ST. GILDAS CLOSE
LANGPORT EASTOVER
BOW STREET
WHATLEY
WHATLEY LANE
WHATLEY HILL
BENNETTS LANE
Huish House
Ch. of B.V.M. Huish
Great Bow Bridge
Rock River
COCKLE MOOR
Rectory
0 100 yards 200 300
0 metres 200

BIBLIOGRAPHY

Michael Aston and Ian Burrow: *The Archaeology of Somerset*
Michael Aston and Roger Leech: *Historic Towns in Somerset*
Mrs. Russell Barrington: *Life of Walter Bagehot*
Robin Bush: *The Victoria History of the County of Somerset. Vol.III*, edited by Robert Dunning
Carter & Mears: *History of Britain*
Chambers' Encyclopaedia
D.P. Dobson M.A.: *The Archaeology of Somerset*
Robert Dunning: *Somerset and Avon*
Robert Dunning, edited by: *The Victoria History of the County of Somerset. Vol.III*
Everyman's Encyclopaedia
Neil Fairbairn: *A Traveller's Guide to the Battlefields of Britain*
Ken Fletcher: *The Somerset Levels and Moors*
Maxwell Fraser: *Companion into Somerset*
Maxwell Fraser: *Somerset*
T.J. Hunt and R.R. Sellman: *Aspects of Somerset History*
Francis A. Knight asstd. by Louie M. Dutton: *Somerset*
D. Melville Ross, M.A.: *Langport and its Church*
A.L. Morton: *A People's History of England*
Ordnance Survey: *Britain in the Dark Ages*
Derek Phillips: *Working Yeovil to Taunton Steam*
Mrs. Cyril Ransome: *First History of England*
G.M. Trevelyan: *History of England*
Alfred T. Warbis: *Fragments of S. Somerset*
Michael Williams: *The Draining of the Somerset Levels*
Isabel Wyatt: *The Book of Huish*

The Old Bookshop

Bow Street, Langport, Somerset TA10 9PQ
Telephone: Langport (0458) 252644

★ **BOOKS** Both second-hand and new, of local interest and on an unusually wide variety of subjects
★ **BOOKS** Bought
★ **BOOKS** Ordered on Request
★ **BOOKS** Searched for
★ **BOOKS** in our Annexe @20p only... plus
★ **ORDNANCE SURVEY MAPS**
★ **SPOKEN WORD CASSETTES**

Open: Monday - Saturday
9.00am to 5.30pm

Prop. Heather Ridgway